Inside Out Transformation™
presents

GETTING GOD™
"The GOD Project"

Inside Out Transformation™
presents

GETTING GOD™
"The GOD Project"

6 Steps for

Divining Your Way to a More

Intimate and Loving Relationship with God

Linda Humphreys, PhD

GETTING GOD™ ~ **"The GOD Project"**
6 Steps for Divining Your Way to a More Intimate and Loving Relationship with God
© 2019 Linda Humphreys, PhD
www.DrLindaHumphreys.com

Published by Inside Out Transformation, LLC

The contents in this book are not meant to diagnose medical and / or psychological problems. Neither the work I do nor the information presented within this book are a substitute for medical attention and care, psychological counseling, and / or psychiatric care. No guarantees or claims are made regarding diagnosing, cures, clearings, releasing, and / or healings.

The information provided in this book is strictly for the purposes of energetic and spiritual awareness. If you choose to apply the ideas provided within this book, you are taking full responsibility for your actions.

Unless otherwise noted, all Bible quotations are from the King James version, accessed through *www.biblehub.com*.

Publisher's Cataloging-in-Publication Data
Names: Humphreys, Linda, author.
Title: Getting God "the GOD project" – 6 steps for divining your way to a more intimate and loving relationship with God / Linda Humphreys PhD.
Description: Includes bibliographical references and index. | Inside Out Transformation, LLC, 2019.
Identifiers: ISBN 978-0-9724161-4-6
Subjects: LCSH God. | Spirituality. | Spiritual life. | BISAC SELF-HELP / Spiritual
Classification: LCC BL624 .H855 2019 | DDC 291.4/4--dc23

Interior Designer: Pam Terry
Editor: Candace Johnson; Proofreader: Robin Quinn
Front Cover Original Illustration Artist: Paitoonpati
Book Cover Designers: Linda Humphreys and Erik Allen
Back Cover Photographer: Melody Barooni

Printed in the United States of America

This book is dedicated to

Seekers,
Believers in redemption,
more than second chances—and choosing again,
Dreamers,
Strivers,
Transformers,
Visionaries,
Way-Showers,
and
Those who persist in the quest of capital "T" Truth
both Within and Throughout—
in everything and everyone.

Yesterday I was clever, so I wanted to change the world.
Today I am wise, so I am changing myself.

— **Rumi**

The day will come when,
after harnessing the ether, the winds, the tides, gravitation,
we shall harness for God the energies of love.
And, on that day, for the second time in the history of the world,
man will have discovered fire.

— **Pierre Teilhard de Chardin**

Contents

PART III
"UNSEEN" FORCES AND INFLUENCES

PART IV
"The GOD PROJECT"

Preface

I am an intuitive coach, metaphysical / energy clearing facilitator, and consultant. I do not diagnose and / or treat medical and / or psychological issues, nor are the contents in this book and the accompanying *Guidebook* meant to diagnose and / or treat these issues. The work I do and the information presented within this book and *GETTING GOD*™ ~ *The Guidebook—Exploration & Conscious Connection Support for Your "GOD Project"* are not a substitute for medical attention and care, psychological counseling, and/or psychiatric care.

I assist with the identification and releasing of hidden or underlying energetic blocks and imbalances. In particular, I work with blocks and imbalances that may contribute to and influence one's emotional and physical energetic and may contribute to one's mental and spiritual issues and challenges.

My goal and intention are to assist you in identifying, clearing, and releasing stuck energy in service to your emotional, physical, mental, energetic, and spiritual well-being. Additionally, I want to help you gain clearer access and connection to your unique Divine Healer within.

No guarantees, but the more you remove energetic blocks and imbalances, the better chance your body, mind, and emotions have to be at optimal and supportive functioning—allowing your True Self to shine through.

How to Get Optimal Results

Being open-minded and open and receptive to healing—for your highest and greatest benefit and for the highest and greatest benefit of everyone on the planet—is key to experiencing optimal results.

I am very clear that God / Spirit / Highest Power / Big Love does the healing work.

What to Expect After a Clearing and Release Session

After a session has been completed, be gentle with yourself because you will be going through a readjustment period. Your energetic system will aim to re-alchemize to a less internally burdened and encumbered state. This readjustment period can last a few days. Some symptoms may include emotional sensitivity, crying, difficulty sleeping, becoming sleepy, need for extra sleep, and vivid dreams. Or you may experience nothing at all.

Although results vary from person to person, these are some of the ways people have benefited from doing their own "GOD Project":

- Greater inner peace
- Stronger sense of connection to God
- Greater feeling of love toward God
- Greater sense of love from God
- Increased awareness of love and loving in general
- Greater compassion for themselves and their journey
- Greater compassion for others and their journey too.

BOTTOM LINE: Be gentle on yourself. Just as you would be extra gentle with yourself after a physical surgery, consider these sessions as a type of energetic "surgery." Allow your system to recalibrate to a "new normal." Rest and drink plenty of water.

Also, establish a mindset of gratitude. Cultivate gratitude for everything and everyone. Everything you have ever experienced has brought to you to this moment—a very fine place to be—and a great moment to begin your "GOD Project."

And so it is.

Introduction

"I just don't get *IT*!" I said, sobbing and trembling before an audience of more than 175 people. "The *IT* I don't get is GOD!"

There. I said it.

At the time I made that statement, I'd spent more than twenty years trying to "figure out" God and my "position" with God by:

- Reading spiritual and psychological self-help books,
- Studying with "healers,"
- Attending therapy sessions,
- Visiting psychics,
- Participating in "healing" retreats, workshops, conferences, and expos,
- Taking classes at various churches,
- Seeking spiritual counseling, and
- Praying with spiritual practitioners.

I finally "fessed up."

The fact that I made that confession after one year of study in a two-year master's degree program in Spiritual Psychology only added to my angst!

"I am in extreme judgment right now," I shared with my teachers (who were also directors of the program), other faculty members, classmates, and program staff and volunteers. "After all, I know this is a *spiritual* psychology program, but I am *not* feeling very *spiritual* at this moment!"

***

I had been told that "issues" are like onions—they have many layers. I felt like I had the "mother" of all onions. At the time, I did what I did best: I got busy. I tried to figure things out some more.

Several years later, with my Spiritual Psychology degree and various certifications of advanced-level healing modalities under my belt, I found myself in yet another spiritually oriented healing course. This time the class was related to finances.

One evening the "nature of God" was being discussed. We were asked to write about how we viewed God. My answer (and I literally and intentionally used the masculine pronoun at that time):

> He is withholding, aloof, can be attentive and responsive at times and not at others. Confusing. Unpredictable. Punitive. A mystery. Pretty darn wily, like Wile E. Coyote and the Wascally Wabbit, if you ask me!

Not again! I thought. I couldn't believe I still felt that way after all of these years! Once again, I felt like I had the "mother" of all onions. Hmm …

Mother of all onions … *mother* …

After I saw what I had written, I realized that my description of God was the exact same description I would use to describe my most psychologically and emotionally influential and challenging parent: my mother.

I envied anyone who experienced God as other than what I described. I felt alone and separated from God and others. I even felt alone and separated from my True Self. I wondered if I was the only one who felt that way.

While a great number of us profess our love for God and the view of "God is Love / God as Love," do we *really*, within our subconscious, hold that as the Truth (with a capital "T")? Do we truly hold "God is Love / God as Love" as a sacred Truth—or is it merely wishful thinking? A hope? A platitude? Something we were taught to say and expected to believe?

Do we truly live our lives in the flow of that Truth? Is what we are manifesting in alignment with that Truth?

In subsequent years, I gave my quest for a more intimate and loving experience of my relationship with God more time, attention, and specific focus. I did this in service to experiencing and feeling more resonance with God. I went within to explore the roots of this core issue, clear and release them, and replace the void with more accurate and affirmative programs and perspectives.

My journey and the development of this program were the basis of my dissertation, "The Multiple Personalities of God: Eliminating Projections, Blocks, and the Fallacy of Unrequited Love Regarding One's Relationship with God." (Though that is most likely the longest dissertation title in history, it sums up my end-result experience of this program—and led to the creation of this book and *GETTING GOD™ ~ The Guidebook—Exploration & Conscious Connection Support for Your "GOD Project."*

Additionally, I decided to incorporate some aspects of the energy-healing modalities I had studied, and I applied them directly to myself and my perceived relationship with God in a regular and focused manner. Plus, through prayer (which I define as *talking to* God), meditation (*listening to* God), and intuition (*consciously connecting with and listening to* God Within), I felt prompted to create a program, with carefully laid-out steps and protocols, that would assist others in clearing and releasing energetic blocks and imbalances to improve their perceived / misperceived relationship with God.

Developing a program required rigorous honesty on my part. I had to dig deeper and longer into my own past to uncover my own misperceptions, blocks, and imbalances—and then clear and release them. Perceiving my own self as a "worst-case scenario," I reasoned: *If this program could work for me, it could certainly work for others.*

I became the guinea pig of my own program. Toward the end of my program, I noticed that my perception of the quality of my relationship with God dramatically transformed in a markedly positive way. My program worked!

Later, I made it a goal and intention to develop a program that people could easily use and support themselves with in clearing and releasing their energetic blocks and imbalances that contributed to a sense of separation / distance between themselves and God.

For those of you who say you know and experience "God is Love / God as Love," you might find what I wrote about God in the financial workshop to be rather sacrilegious. After devoting so much effort to being a "good girl" my entire life, the last thing I wanted was to be perceived as sacrilegious. I believe that what I shared was merely what was residing within my subconscious. I believe it came to my conscious awareness to be cleared and released.

Knowing that, as humans, we all have subconscious / unconscious beliefs, I knew that while some people may not harbor the exact same thoughts, feelings, or misperceptions that I share, everyone has their own subconscious programs unconsciously influencing them and their perceptions. We all hold misconceptions and misperceptions within our subconscious, and they do influence our thinking, our actions, our entire lives—including the perceived quality of life and relationships we are experiencing.

I first shared my program with a friend of mine by testing her conscious and subconscious beliefs. Though she swore she did not harbor the same judgments, feelings, and resentments toward God that she was harboring against her father (her most influential parental figure), her subconscious revealed that she did.

I found the same results in every person I tested.

As a "metaphysical scientist" and practitioner of the metaphysical healing arts (some call it *energy medicine*), I am delighted to report that every client I have used this program with has experienced a profound improvement in their perception of the quality of their relationship with God. With the sharing of my challenges and "recovery" with others came more people willing to admit their own personal challenges and frustrations about their perceived relationship with God.

A Universal Issue

In doing the literary research for both my dissertation and this book, what became clear to me is that Roman Catholics (or Catholics, in general) do not have a monopoly on the points I have drawn as they relate to the multiple and conflicting depictions of the nature of God. Although I feature a lot of materials from the Roman Catholic teachings, I believe the challenge of one's perception or misperception of their relationship with God is both universal and pandemic. "Sinners in the Hands of an Angry God," a sermon I quote from in this book, is a Protestant sermon. The King James Bible, which I quote heavily in this book, is the go-to among Protestant ministers and lay people (according to conversations with Protestant ministers and self-reported members of the Protestant faith).

Using the information, tools, and techniques found in *GETTING GOD™ ~ "The GOD Project"—6 Steps for Divining Your Way to a More Intimate & Loving Relationship with God* and *GETTING GOD™ ~ The Guidebook—Exploration & Conscious Connection Support for Your "GOD Project"* an assist in clearing the way for the True Nature of God to be explored, revealed, and experienced. This can release dissonance and allow for a more enriched perceived experience of and relationship with God—and ultimately with yourself and others.

This book in *not* about mother, father, or religion bashing. It is intended to assist you in looking at how you perceive God and how you perceive your relationship with God. It is offered as a tool to assist you in exploring your conscious and subconscious / unconscious beliefs about God. It is also intended to provide you with assistance in releasing a perceived sense of separation between you and God—your Highest Good. It can also assist you in releasing negative energy you may be harboring against your parents, boss, coworkers, yourself ... anyone.

This book *is* one that provides an easy and supportive way in which to explore, uncover, and clear and release unconscious /

subconscious energy, thoughts, blocks, imbalances, and vibrations that do not serve you. It is intended to assist you in recognizing, owning, and allowing your highest and best God-Self to shine through.

Each and every step is specifically designed to support your system (body, psyche, mind, energy field, and so on) with specific steps and protocols that, if followed, support a gentle clearing and releasing process that can yield maximum transformative results. It was my intention to focus on the *practical* nature of the work rather than the science behind it. Resources are provided for you to delve deeper into the science of it all if you wish to pursue more in-depth research.

Within these pages you will learn about *divining* and about aligning with the Divine to accomplish what the poet and mystic Jalal ad-Din Mohammad Rumi wrote about in the following quote:

> Your task is not to seek for love, but merely to seek and find all the barriers within yourself that you have built against it.

This book and the accompanying **Guidebook** offer support in seeking and finding all the barriers you have built against Love—God as Love—and clearing and releasing them from within.

As I mentioned earlier, healing is often described as the unpeeling of a multilayered onion. It can also be like the removing of the prickly leaves of an artichoke to ultimately reveal the soft heart inside. May what is provided within these pages assist you in removing your multilayered, prickly parts to reveal the beautiful, soft, tender, loving heart inside you and inside each and every one of us—the beautiful, loving heart of God.

It is time for you to get out of your own way and release any and all sense of victimhood—on all levels. Celebrate and embrace your Good, your Loving, your God Within you and within all others.

It is time for you to be *"GETTING GOD."*

PART I

MY EXPLORATION

Chapter 1

In the Beginning …

Our conscious motivations, ideas, and beliefs are a blend of false information, biases, irrational passions, rationalizations, prejudices, in which morsels of truth swim around and give the reassurance, albeit false, that the whole mixture is real and true.

—Erich Fromm

I decided it was important for me to explore what I had been exposed to as I was growing up regarding the nature of God in different forms of media (books, texts, movies, and song). I conducted a thorough investigation into what, exactly, I was exposed to and what, exactly, I took in—both consciously and subconsciously—about who—and what—God was.

While I had other forms of religious training (Sunday school, Saturday catechism, church sermons), I found how God was portrayed in media to be especially impactful.

The possible reasons for the lasting impact are varied: Perhaps it was the age at which I was exposed to the medium; the graphic illustrations in the religious books that filled a bookcase in the home I grew up in; and the repetition in which I saw or heard things (illustrations, movies, and songs). The repetitive nature of watching the same movies, reading the same books (the Bible, *Baltimore Catechism*), and singing the same songs over and over again reinforced and entrenched any and all emotional reactions, negative or otherwise, that I experienced. Another potential reason: The experience of watching movies (and I would venture to also say listening to music—and even looking at illustrations in written texts) involves multi-sensory stimulation, which reinforces any emotional reaction I might have experienced while being exposed to the materials.

As an adult, simply doing the research and being exposed to the same materials I grew up with, I felt as if I was reliving the same emotions I experienced as a child, including two prominent emotions—confusion and fear. Quite often, while conducting my research and reviewing the materials, I cried from the emotional impact.

Characteristics of God

As many things that are spiritually based stem from the Bible, my research began there. While exploring the Old Testament, I noticed that God was described in various terms in numerous passages:

Jealous

> For thou shalt worship no other god: for the LORD, whose name *is* Jealous, *is* a jealous God. (Exod 34:14)

> For the LORD thy God *is* a consuming fire, *even* a jealous God. (Dt 4: 24)

> (For the LORD thy God *is* a jealous God among you) lest the anger of the LORD thy God be kindled against thee, and destroy thee from off the face of the earth. (Dt 6:15)

Angry

> And the anger of the LORD was kindled against them; and he departed. (Nm 12:9)

> How long, LORD? wilt thou be angry for ever? shall thy jealousy burn like fire? (Ps 79:5)

> Wilt thou be angry with us for ever? wilt thou draw out thine anger to all generations? (Ps 85:5)

Vengeful and Punishing

> And the LORD said unto Moses, Take all the heads of the

people, and hang them up before the LORD against the sun, that the fierce anger of the LORD may be turned away from Israel. (Nm 25:4)

And the LORD'S anger was kindled against Israel, and he made them wander in the wilderness forty years, until all the generation, that had done evil in the sight of the LORD, was consumed. (Nm 32:13)

The LORD will not spare him, but then the anger of the LORD and his jealousy shall smoke against that man, and all the curses that are written in this book shall lie upon him, and the LORD shall blot out his name from under heaven. (Dt 29:20)

Thou shalt not bow down thyself unto them, nor serve them: for I the LORD thy God *am* a jealous God, visiting the iniquity of the fathers upon the children unto the third and fourth *generation* of them that hate me (9), and shewing mercy unto thousands of them that love me and keep my commandments (10). (Dt 5:9-10)

The above quotes are just a blush of what can be found. There are many other passages that could be quoted. I chose just a few to illustrate my point.

The following is in Galatians 5:19-21 in the Lamsa Bible's New Testament:

For the works of the flesh are well known, which are these: adultery, impurity, and lasciviousness, idolatry, witchcraft, enmity, strife, jealousy, anger, stubbornness, seditions, heresies, envyings, murders, drunkenness, revellings, and all such things; those who practice these things, as I have told you before and I say to you now, shall not inherit the kingdom of God.

The contradiction I see here is that "jealousy" and "anger" are deemed qualities that are not fit for those who hope to "inherit the kingdom of God"—yet God, as you can see from the biblical references cited above, is extremely jealous and prone to fits of anger— even rage!

Wrath is one of "The Seven Deadly Sins." BibleInfo.com defines wrath as "uncontrollable feelings of anger and hate toward another person." If we continue to use the Bible as a resource into the nature of God, it appears that God is extremely prone to wrath as well.

The Wrath of God
Apparently, according to the Bible, God is extremely vengeful and punitive.

> And Moses besought the LORD his God, and said, LORD, why doth thy wrath wax hot against thy people, which thou hast brought forth out of the land of Egypt with great power, and with a mighty hand? (Ex 32:11)

> And while the flesh *was* yet between their teeth, ere it was chewed, the wrath of the LORD was kindled against the people, and the LORD smote the people with a very great plague. (Ex 11:33)

> And the LORD rooted them out of their land in anger, and in wrath, and in great indignation, and cast them into another land, as *it is* this day. (Ex 29:28)

Fear of God
Having a fear of God is reinforced in Roman Catholicism. According to the catechism books I grew up with, such as in *Baltimore Catechism No. 1*, one of the seven "Virtues and Gifts of the Holy Spirit" is "fear of God."

The God of Israel said, the Rock of Israel spake to me, He that ruleth over men *must be* just, ruling in the fear of God. (2 Sm 23:3)

Submitting yourselves one to another in the fear of God. (Eph 5:21)

Additionally, the Bible states:

And the spirit of the Lord shall rest upon him; the spirit of wisdom and of understanding, the spirit of counsel and of fortitude, the spirit of knowledge and of godliness. And he shall be filled with the spirit of the fear of the Lord. (Is 11:2-3)

Additional Sources of Confusion

In one of my public high school English classes we had to read a sermon written by British Colonial theologian Jonathan Edwards, first presented in 1741, titled "Sinners in the Hands of an Angry God."

This sermon was extremely impactful for me. It was another example of God's anger—and added another reason to fear God. In my mind, it conjured vivid images of hell, damnation, fear—and even terror of God. One of the most memorable quotes is: "There is nothing that keeps wicked Men at any one Moment, out of Hell, but the mere Pleasure of GOD."

After reading this sermon, not only did I perceive God as angry, jealous, vengeful, and wrath-prone, but I got the clear and distinct impression that God was wickedly sadistic! I felt and thought that God was always toying with me—hanging the threat of death with eternal damnation in hell over me; my eternal fate was always precariously hanging in the balance by a thread. I felt I had to please God ... or I was a *goner*. It appeared that I would never stand a chance with God. God was always waiting for me to fail, and no matter what I did, I would fail. I would always fall short and land in the "sinner" category, which would take me straight to hell. I felt I was damned—and doomed to perpetually have to "walk on eggshells."

Around that same time in high school, I came across a poster featuring names and descriptions of God that appeared in the Bible. Though the poster listed some of what I would label "gentle" and "loving" qualities and names for God, because of my already deeply rooted perception of feeling confused and afraid of God, I focused on terms such as "warrior," "vanquisher," "reprover," and "conqueror."

Finding a similar graphic on the internet, what struck me was how bipolar some of the names and terms were; they were polar opposites. Below is an example of some of the contradictions that struck me:

Lion of the Tribe of Judah	Lamb
Destroyer	Repairer
Warrior	Gate
Reprover	Advocate
Unmovable	Fountain
Vanquisher	Light
Conqueror	Rescuer

These kinds of contradictory terms only bolstered my confusion. Each column had a very different feeling and tone, and as I would learn later, a different vibration.

Another source of confusion (and a perceived sense of separation) came from my family and the religion into which I was born and raised. *Baltimore Catechism* was the standard and the go-to source for all Roman Catholic doctrine and dogma at the time I grew up. A majority of the text is done in a question and answer format. Book 1, Lesson 1 is titled "The Purpose of Man's Existence," and it reads:

2. Who is God?
God is the Supreme Being who made all things.

3. Why did God make us?
God made us to show forth His goodness and to share with us His everlasting happiness in heaven.

4. What must we do to gain the happiness of heaven?
To gain the happiness of heaven we must learn how to know, love, and serve God in this world.

In Lesson 2, "God And His Perfections," God is described as follows:

8. What do we mean when we say that God is the Supreme Being?
When we say that God is the Supreme Being we mean that He is above all creatures.

Determined to find some semblance of something "warm and fuzzy," I did a word search for *love*. Love was only directed *toward* God; it never came *from* God. An example of this one-sided love is found in Lesson 10, "The Virtues and Gifts of the Holy Spirit":

63. What is charity?
Charity is the virtue by which we love God above all things for His own sake, and our neighbor as ourselves for the love of God.

Sadly, even in Lesson 35, "Matrimony," there was nary a mention of the word *love*.

Another, somewhat child-friendly (as this one had colorful illustrations) go-to book for me was *The New Saint Joseph First Communion Catechism* (1963). In Lesson 1, titled "God Made Us," it does state: "He [sic: God] made me because He loves me." However, the dogma does revert back to love ... going in the direction of God.

4. What must I do to be happy with God in heaven?
To be happy with God in heaven I must know Him, love Him, and serve Him in this world.

If one were to measure the amount of love discussed and featured within these texts compared to the amount of loving and serving we have to do for God, one might fall prey to the perception of unrequited love. With so much given and with, at best, uncertain results, I believe it is clear to see how one could easily feel frustrated with and grow leery of God. (That was, at least, the case for me.)

Another Roman Catholic catechism book is *Sister Annunziata's First Communion Catechism*. Though more catering to children, the message is basically the same. Before the title page is this message:

> *Dear Boys and Girls:*
> *When the baby JESUS was born in Bethlehem, He was THINKING about each one of you. He LOVED each one of you. JESUS wants YOU to THINK about Him. He wants YOU to LOVE Him. He wants YOU to OBEY Him. He wants YOU to receive Him in HOLY COMMUNION ...*

This seems to set a more "warm and fuzzy" tone. However, the dogma and doctrine is simply too prominent, and the one-way directionality of love is, once again, the central theme. This is from Lesson 1, titled "The Purpose of Man's Existence":

What God Wants Me To Do
I must know God because He made me.
I can best know God through the Catholic Church.
The Catholic Church tells me all about God.
I must love God because He is all-good.
When I am good, I show God that I love Him.
I must serve God.
I serve God when I do what He tells me to do.
God wants me to go to heaven.
I want to go to heaven.
I want to be happy forever with God.

With this type of text, I gleaned that not only did I have to serve God, but I felt as if I had to prove my love through service as well. It seemed as if I was required to prove to God that I loved "Him" vis-à-vis "show[ing] God that I love Him."

With all of my efforts (that is, loving, serving, and proving something to God), and in spite of "waiting for the other shoe to fall," I tried to garner favor with God lest I displease "Him" and "He" sends me to hell at any moment, as Jonathan Edwards threatened. I was scared, tired, confused, and frustrated, and I felt quite desolate.

Who We Are to God

Curious to know what God thought of us and how others perceived themselves as it related to God, I continued my research. Finding what I did only amplified my feelings of distance from God *and* made me want to distance myself from God. Quite frankly, what I discovered made me want to even hide from God.

Worms

The term *worm* and the notion of being a worm and / or being equated as such is found in the following Bible verses:

> How much less man, *that is* a **worm**? and the son of man, *which is* a worm? (Jb 25:6)

> But I *am* a worm, and no man; a reproach of men, and despised of the people. (Ps 22:6)

To make matters even worse (according to the King James version of the Bible), the following verse says that God not only thinks of us as worms, but God even calls us (or at least calls Jacob) a "worm."

> Fear not, thou worm Jacob, *and* ye men of Israel; I will help thee, saith the LORD, and thy redeemer, the Holy One of Israel. (Is 41:14)

Jacob was loved by God (Mal 1:3). If God felt that Jacob was a *worm* and even called him such—that further compounded my feelings of being set up to experience a losing proposition—and only to get punished for it. The deck was not stacked in my favor. As a matter of fact, I definitely felt as if God deliberately and intentionally stacked the deck against me. This caused me to wonder—What the heck does God think of *me*? Even worse—What the heck will God *do* to me?

"A Wretch"

One of the most popular and familiar Christian songs is "Amazing Grace." When singing that song, we reinforce that a person is merely "a wretch."

Amazing Grace
Amazing Grace how sweet the sound
That saved a wretch like me …
—John Newton

Dictionary.com defines *wretch* as:

1. a deplorably unfortunate or unhappy person,

2. a person of despicable or base character.

Furthermore, *despicable* is defined as "deserving to be despised, or regarded with distaste, disgust, or disdain; contemptible."

What About Your Religious Upbringing?

While reading the citations you have just read, some of my friends and clients had these comments:

"Oh my gosh! I read the same text—and I felt the same way!"

"I never heard of that book. Glad I was never exposed to *that*!"

"I thought *I* was the only one who felt that way—and I was too embarrassed to admit it!"

"It's no wonder you were so 'challenged with God'! Look at what you grew up with! Look at what you were exposed to!"

"Reading this touched something deep within me. I never thought I had a 'challenge' or block in this [God] department of my life. Now I realize, I have had a distant and strained relationship with God my entire life. I never would have thought I did—or at least I never thought I would admit to it—until now …"

Perhaps ideas like these came up within you too.

You might ask yourself:

- What was I taught about God?

- As a child, how did this make me feel?

- Do I now believe what I was taught?

- Do I now feel the same way toward God that I did as a child?

While **GETTING GOD**™ ~ *"The GOD Project"* does not heavily focus time and attention on the mental level and its constructs, I believe that addressing *all* levels, including the mental, is imperative for holistic transformation and transcendence.

I also believe it is important to explore and note your emotional reactions to your initial religious training because within reactions lie the seeds of initial judgments and misperceptions about the True Nature of God and, ultimately, of ourselves and others. Addressing judgments is like following breadcrumbs that lead to the path of discovering your conscious and subconscious programming.

Chapter 2

"Evidence" of Separation:
My Story and My Quest

*It's not what happens to you, but how you react
to it that matters.*

—Epictetus

Given that I perceived God as being precarious, temperamental, cruel, mean, punitive, and angry, I wondered, *Was God loving?* One minute God is one thing, another minute something else. In my study of psychology, I learned the combination of these personality traits and / or behaviors are associated with schizophrenia, multiple personality disorders, mood disorders, and bipolar disorder, to name a few.

Does God have multiple personalities? Is God schizophrenic? Does God have a mood disorder? Is God bipolar? Or are all the contradictions and depictions merely authors' projections of their own multiple personalities, fears, anger, or bipolar or schizophrenic nature—and projected onto God?

I tried hard to understand, connect, and feel ... God. Always feeling like something was missing, I read books, attended seminars, retreats, programs, webinars and metaphysical expos, sought out healers, channelers, mediums, and clairvoyants, worked with angels and spirit guides, and tried various healing modalities—just to name a few of the avenues I pursued. It seemed that no matter how much I effort I put in, I only become more frustrated, disillusioned, and deflated. Also, in spite of all of my efforts, I felt an even greater—and ever-increasing—sense of separation between myself and God.

Guilt—Roman Catholic-style blended with New Age-style—was ever-present. My Roman Catholic side's inner tirade would go something like this: *I am sinner. God is too busy right now. Pray to Mary. Oh, she is probably too busy too. I should pray to one of the saints. I should go to confession. I need to go to communion. I do not want to end up in hell or purgatory. Why isn't God there? Why isn't God blessing me? Why isn't 'He' listening to me?*

My New Age side's inner tirade would be something like this: *Because I am personally responsible for everything that manifests or does not manifest in my life, what is in my own consciousness that causes this 'strained' relationship? What the heck is wrong with me? I am trying my best to love God. Why am I not loved back? I am affirming, visualizing, meditating, lighting candles and incense, and praying. Am I doing it wrong? I am grateful! Am I not grateful enough? Why am I doing this to myself? Why doesn't God intervene? Where is God?*

A common theme and thread of energy that I detected in both styles of guilt, and that I was using against myself, went like this: *Why am I being punished? What am I doing wrong? Why is God withholding from me?* Even more prominent was: *What is wrong with me?*

My "Relationship Project"

When I was pursuing a master's degree in Spiritual Psychology at the University of Santa Monica (USM), one of the course's requirements was called a "Relationship Project." We were supposed to pick our most challenging relationship—the relationship to which we would say, "No! Not *that* relationship!" It could also be the one relationship that, if it could be "healed," would make the most significant and positive impact in our life. Without one moment of hesitation, I knew the object of my relationship project: GOD.

Getting approval to have "God" as the subject / object of my relationship project was a bit of a challenge. However, based on some things I had shared in the past within the program, as well as seeing my determination, the program directors approved "God" as the focus of my project.

Investigating the Sources of My Separation

I explored my memory to trace the root cause of my pervasive sense of separation from God. I began by looking into the religion I was born and raised in as well as the belief system (programs) that was instilled in me while I was growing up.

The Baltimore Catechism and other Bible-based picture books, featuring God as an old man with a white beard, sitting on a throne in the clouds and holding a lightning bolt, are some of the sources of separation that came to mind. Digging deeper, I remembered an image from a movie I saw that literally scared the bejesus out of me.

- The movie: *The Ten Commandments.*

- The scene: Lot and his family leaving Sodom and Gomorrah.

- What impacted me: God turning Lot's wife (nameless other than "Lot's wife") into salt. If that was not bad enough, her nose and her arms fell off too.

Through the eyes of a child, that scene was terrifying and disturbing, to say the very least. It literally left an indelible impression on me. My reasoning: *If God would do that to Lot's wife, what the heck will God do to me?*

I tried my best to be "good." I tried my best to be a good Roman Catholic. I tried my best to follow the rules. I tried my best to follow all of the dogma. I tried my best to follow all of the rituals.

I tried.

Another Source of Separation

Looking within, and upon reflection of my own experience, in addition to the indoctrination I received through the aforementioned books, movie, and song (plus others), I realized that I also learned about God through another extremely close and personal source: my mother.

To describe my mother's personality as angry would not even do it justice. However, for a lack of a better word, suffice it to say she was angry at everything and everyone—especially God.

My mother's unrelenting mantras were "God never listens to me," "God never answers my prayers," and "God never gives me what I want." She verbalized these, plus a myriad of similar statements and sentiments, constantly.

One day I was asked by a neighbor (let's call her Nancy) how my mother was. I told her that my mother was sad. When asked why, I shared with Nancy one of my mother's daily mantras. What I shared got back to my mother, and she was infuriated. She told me to go up to my bedroom and kneel before a religious calendar; I was then ordered to pray to God to beg for forgiveness and to beg God not to send me to hell. That day I received the most severe physical beating I have ever experienced growing up—a beating for telling the truth. The physical pain was nothing compared to the terror and confusion I experienced toward God—and the foreboding sense of being eternally punished for having told the truth to an adult / authority figure when asked.

I was about four years old. I had told the truth. I wondered, *Would telling the truth lead to being punished by God and result in being sent to hell? Should I continue to tell the truth—and would I continue to be punished for it? Why would God send me to hell?* I was confused—and frightened of God. Looking back, I was always "walking on eggshells" in fear of "the other shoe falling," always looking over my shoulder, tip-toeing my way through life, and in fear that God would get angry at me at any given moment and send me to hell—or equally bad, turn me into salt like Lot's wife.

My approximately four-year-old brain wired the following together:

Telling the Truth → God being mad at me + God punishing me = Eternal hell, fire, and damnation

While I am now, as an adult, reflecting, examining, and "using my words" regarding a situation I experienced as a child, who—at that time—did not have the words nor the capacity to "use my words," examine, decipher, and label my thought processes, this incident did have a *huge* impact on me. These are the emotional, mental, psychological, and spiritual imprints I experienced as they related to God:

God is scary.

I am bad.

I will be punished.

My Separation, Continued

In later years, my form of young-adult rebellion was joining what I now look back on and view as a Christian cult. We lived in "households" and were "shepherded" (that is, guided what to do, what not to do, and so on) by others called "church elders." Anytime I asked a question of the elders, they always quoted Bible verses to me.

Being born and raised a Roman Catholic and having attended Catechism (Catholic Sunday school), I was never really exposed to the Bible per se, other than Bible verses that were read every Sunday by the priest from the pulpit. There were never any Bibles in the pews—only "Sunday Missals" with some Bible excerpts included. At the time I lived in the *household*, I was quite intimidated by not being able to spout Bible verses. Everyone around me in my new church was more Bible "literate." I felt not as "Christian" or "as good of a Christian" as they were.

After some time, I felt called to leave that church and household and venture out. I informed the church elders about my decision. I was told—actually warned—not to leave. I told the elders, "I know what I want to do with my life—and it is not to stay here." Their reply was "We know God." After reciting a myriad of Bible verses, they told me I should stay or I would suffer the consequences—which would lead to "hell and eternal damnation."

I left. I felt separate and apart from God. I felt deep sadness—even depression, and a lot more confusion. From that time until I began to explore my perceived / misperceived relationship with God (in service to "improving" it), my feelings toward God were these: *You stay over there and I'll stay way over here. Please don't hit me with a lightning bolt. I will be way over here trying to be good.*

Throughout my life I heard people make statements such as "I always knew that God loved me," "I feel so close to God," and "God is always with me." I was envious. I was angry that I did not have that. What I had always wanted was a close, personal, intimate experience and relationship with God. As a character says in the movie *When Harry Met Sally*, "I want what she is having." I was determined to turn my perceived relationship with God around.

During the course of the seven-month Relationship Project in graduate school, I did, indeed, experience great epiphanies, revelations, healings, and blessings. I owe a debt of gratitude to the directors of the program for allowing me to pursue the "healing" of this relationship.

The end of my project culminated with a creative poster-board collage. On one side, I pasted images of God as I perceived God to be while I was growing up and prior to the start of the Project. Some of the images included a picture of King Kong raging on top of the Empire State Building, a nun with a ruler in her hand—scolding someone, the Tasmanian Devil, Dr. Jekyll and Mr. Hyde, the Phantom of the Opera, and an exploding atomic bomb, just to name a few. The other side of the poster was named "The New Faces of God." On that side of the poster, I made a collage of the following: pictures of my friends, flowers, sunsets, sunrises, rainbows, nature, and so on. My new symbol / image of God became a photograph taken by NASA of a nebula, which I placed in the center of the poster.

In spite of all of the gifts I received as a result of the "Relationship Project" assignment and graduate program, I knew there were more blocks and barriers within me that prevented me from experiencing the richness and fullness of a relationship with God. I realized that there still might be elements of my "story" that I was using as "evidence"—evidence of separation between myself and God. I believed there was more opportunity and greater potential of having a more loving perception and intimate experience of my relationship with God.

I persevered.

Chapter 3

Conscious and Unconscious Perceptions and Projections

Unless we are possessed of an unusual degree of self-awareness we shall never see through our projections but must always succumb to them, because the mind in its natural state presupposes the existence of such projections. It is the natural and given thing for unconscious contents to be projected.

—Carl Jung

Looking back on my childhood, I would judge my mother to be "withholding"—just like her version of God. I felt the same way about my mother that she felt about God. My judgments toward her included: *She never listens to me, She never responds to my requests, She never gives me what I want, She is never there for me,* and *She is always sad.*

My mother, a child of two Roman Catholic immigrants from Europe, was taught to have "blind faith" about everything relating to her religion. When I questioned her about what she would call "Articles of Faith," she would always tell me to ask one of the priests in our church. If I told her I did not want to know what any of the priests said and wanted to know what she thought and felt about things, she would just tell me she had "blind faith" about everything. My mother tried to instill that same type of unquestioning "blind faith" within me.

While my mother lived her life in anger against God, I always wanted and strived for something new—something better, different—and kinder and gentler. I wanted to experience God as loving.

GETTING GOD™ ~ "The GOD Project"

Perceptions

My beliefs, thoughts, and judgments about my mother, as a parent, greatly affected my perceived relationship with my "Heavenly Parents": God / "Our Father" / "Heavenly Father" and Mary / "Mother Mary" / "Heavenly Mother."

Every time I had to do a confessional penance, I was ordered by the priest to say lots of the "Our Father" and "Hail Mary" prayers and ordered to "beg Mother Mary for forgiveness"—in addition to begging Heavenly Father *and* Jesus for their forgiveness too. Especially after receiving the beating (with religious overtones) from my mother (described in Chapter 2), I did not want to approach nor be anywhere near *any* mother who I had to appease and "walk on eggshells" around—even a "heavenly" mother—*especially* Mary.

Looking back, the reason is quite clear. As a child, I reasoned that while my earthly mother could beat me, Mary could—if not send me to hell herself—tell God (the angry old guy with the lightning bolt) to send me to hell. If that did not work, Mary could also convince her son Jesus to condemn me to eternal hell and damnation. That made Mary just as scary as God—and even *more* scary because she could play both ends against the middle—*me!*

I felt doomed.

In my quest to find the "capital T" Truth, I persevered. Determined to experience a more loving relationship with God, I pressed on. I began studying metaphysics (meaning beyond the physical). I felt an "awakening" and a strong calling to clear any and all blocks within (meaning judgments, attitudes, negative thinking, emotions that felt trapped within me, and so on) which hindered my ability to experience a loving and intimate relationship with God. I no longer wanted to accept anyone else's "truth." I wanted to find my own "Truth."

I made a list of the blocks that still lingered in my conscious awareness, as they related to my perceptions and feelings toward

24

God. The list was not pretty. It contained some of the following impressions I experienced as a little girl after being exposed to all of the dogma and doctrine. The list was also influenced by—and reflected—the punitive religious atmosphere in which I grew up. My list looked like this:

- My relationship with God is …
    - *strained,*
    - *estranged,*
    - *distant, and*
    - *sporadic,*
    - *confusing,*
    - *challenging.*

God is …
    - *wanting to punish me,*
    - *not there when I need support,*
    - *aloof,*
    - *withholding.*

As an adult, keeping in mind the concept of projections and knowing that I (essentially) get (at least energetically and vibrationally) what I give out, I turned the tables on myself. Somewhere within me, I harbored the exact same characteristics. This is what my projects list looked like:

- I am …
    - *wanting to punish myself,*
    - *not there for myself when I need internal support,*
    - *aloof toward myself,*
    - *withholding from myself.*

Speaking of *turning the tables*, truth be told, God could probably say the same of my side of the relationship. *However,* God would never and could never do so because that would go against God's True Nature, which is pure and unconditionally loving. (More about that to come.)

Wanting to grow past this, I pursued my quest with greater intensity—digging even deeper. I searched for books, workshops, teachers—something … anything—that would help me make sense of God. During this time, I discovered the book *Conversations With God: An Uncommon Dialogue, Book 1* by Neale Donald Walsch.

After reading a few pages, I put the book down and sobbed. I do not remember the exact line or paragraph that struck me. What I remember is realizing two extraordinary things: First, I shared some of Walsch's same frustrations and questions. I had a lot of "why" questions for God myself. Second, I was deeply touched by God's responses to Walsch's questions. What I experienced while reading a brief passage had an intense and profound effect on me.

I began to wonder the following: What if all of the stories, theories, belief systems, and theologies about God were all (literally) *man*-made concoctions? What if none of them were: (a) true at all; and (b) certainly not the (capital T) Truth? What if they were merely false stories that were assigned and attributed to God—and handed down through the centuries? What if everything I ever heard, was taught, read, and believed actually had nothing to do with the Truth of God and God's True Nature?

These queries, and the subsequent revelations, hit me like a ton of bricks. Once again, I sobbed. I felt duped by all of what I had been taught by "religion"—especially about God. Eager to find and release core blocks that supported and upheld my stories, thoughts, and feelings of a perceived separation between God and me, I pressed on.

Projections

I remembered that in my undergraduate degree study of psychology, graduate studies in Spiritual Psychology, and advanced graduate studies in Consciousness, Health, and Healing (CHH), the topic of "projections" was discussed and explored.

Projections, as defined in Jungian terms, are "an automatic process whereby contents of one's own unconscious are perceived to be in others." In his book *Dreams*, Jung writes:

> All the contents of our unconscious are constantly being projected into our surroundings, and it is only by recognizing certain properties of the objects as projections or images that we are able to distinguish them from the real properties of the objects.

Another Carl Jung quote came to mind: "I am not what happened to me, I am what I choose to become." I questioned what I was consciously—and *subconsciously*—choosing to become.

I wondered if I was projecting my personality qualities and characteristics onto God. Was I projecting things onto God that had nothing to do with God?

I learned that unconscious / subconscious projections can be negative and / or positive in nature. With this in mind, I decided to concentrate on embracing the characteristics of new positive projections—both from within (myself) and throughout (involving everyone and everything). In addition to taking active measures to clear any and all blocks and negative subconscious programs within, I was also determined and committed to fully recognizing, owning, embracing and expressing these positive qualities.

Consequences of Conscious and Subconscious Negative Perceptions

Negative emotions—and, I would add, persistent negative thinking—can influence your emotional state and become lodged in your energy field. After a period of time, if not identified and removed, this stuck, dense energy can distort your energy field. Energy distortion may also lead to physical challenges and symptoms—to give one example.

Because everything is made of energy, any type of distortion within an energy field—whether it is a negative thought and / or emotion—may lead to negative consequences and distortions on *all* levels: physical, mental, emotional, psychological, spiritual, energetic, and so on.

There are many reasons why and circumstances in which we could experience sadness, anxiety, and / or depression during our lives: severe illness, loss of a job, loss of a home, finances, failing grades in school, death of a family member, separation and divorce, and experiencing a sense of isolation are just a few examples.

We can also experience fear, stress, and loneliness. Most of the time, these internal states diminish and fade away after a period of time. If, however, they linger—and perhaps even intensify to the point of interfering with daily life—this may be a sign of depression and / or an anxiety disorder.

The effects of long-term depression and an anxiety disorder on someone's life, as well as on the lives of those around that person, can be profound. This can contribute to enhanced feelings and perceptions of isolation and separation from others, society, the world—and from God.

My Experience

Depression, persistent and pervasive feelings of shame, guilt, anger, and feeling lost and forlorn with a deep sense of separation (from within myself, my family, others, and God) were ever-present in my life. As these increased and intensified, my own will to live diminished.

Though I was trained, on the mental level, that God was always with me and was a source of love and strength, I felt that somehow that information never reached my heart. My mind would say that my heart felt "broken." I felt that *I* was broken, damaged, and doomed. I felt lost and even "forsaken" by God. Somewhere along the line, I felt that I had forsaken myself.

Having people tell me, "Think positive thoughts!" and "What do you have to be sad about? God loves you!" and similar comments, though well meaning, were *not* helpful at all. They only contributed to what was already an intensely frustrating situation. While those statements might have been true, at that time they were not a Truth for me. Focusing on these messages only served as another weapon in my already-filled-to-the-brim arsenal that I used to beat myself up with.

Actually, it was my thinking mind that was beating me up. A sense (impression, idea, sensation) that something was wrong would trigger my mind. (Usually the something that was "wrong" was within me. Actually, the something "wrong" was usually perceived *as* me, because I was told that almost daily and, as a child, I internalized that message.)

The triggering of my thinking mind would launch a cycle or loop of me thinking—and believing—that something was amiss. My mind would then react by trying to figure things out (the thinking mind's specialty) and would then label my reactions as *negative* emotions. My mind would then search for, find, and attach a story to my *negative* emotions within its memory files that would keep my thinking mind engaged and hooked. All of this served to fuel and perpetuate my negative story / stories.

Additionally, my body would respond to my negative emotions and thoughts. If I was not emotionally depressed, I was mentally depressed. This also contributed to experiencing physical (chemical) depression. My body produced negative physiological responses to my negative thinking, negative stories, and negative emotions.

BOTTOM LINE: I created a vicious cycle within myself. If I was chemically depressed, I would become emotionally depressed. If I was not chemically or emotionally depressed, I was mentally depressed. This cycle became a habit. This habit became a perpetual cycle / loop in my life. I felt and thought that cycle / loop was to be the sum total of my life's experience. My future seemed rather dark and bleak.

I finally began to realize that if I had subconscious / unconscious (or even conscious) negative thoughts, stories, and emotions that were affecting my entire being, there must be a way to decipher their root. I wanted to unlearn my negative patterns by removing and replacing my negative thoughts and emotions with something more positive, supportive, and uplifting. I wanted to alter, in a positive way, my entire being and experience of life.

Determined to unravel the blocks and imbalances I created within, I pressed on.

PART II

MY EPIPHANIES and INSIGHTS

Chapter 4

Epiphanies

There are no mistakes, no coincidences.
All events are blessings given to us to learn from.

—Elisabeth Kübler-Ross

Before I begin any clearing / releasing session, including my own, I meditate to become a clear channel and attune to my inner listening skills. I also say a prayer, state my healing intention, and ask for the assistance of God / Spirit / Highest Power.

During one of my own subconscious / unconscious clearing sessions, the following transpired:

1. I closed my eyes, took a deep breath, and connected with my heart.

   My request: "Please clearly bring forward whatever can be easily and gently released as it relates to this issue and whatever, after clearing and releasing it, will make a significant and positive difference in my healing and in my life."

   Answer: "God scares me."

2. Wanting more information, as I wanted to get to the core, the root of this issue, I asked within:

   Q: "Is there another image or program that is contributing to the program of feeling that 'God is scary'?"

   A: "Yes."

3. I asked God to reveal it to me.

The image of Lot's wife being turned into salt came to mind.

Q: "Is there another?"

A: "Yes."

4. I asked God / Spirit / My Highest Power to reveal it to me.

What came forward was an image I remembered seeing at a very young age, which came from another Bible-inspired movie. Additionally, the story and script were taken word for word from the King James version of the Bible, which served to reinforce the image, words, and message I had taken in.

- The image: Jesus dying on the cross.

- The Bible verses: "And about the ninth hour Jesus cried out with a loud voice, saying, "Eli, Eli, lama sabachthani?" that is, "My God, My God, why have You forsaken Me?" (Mt 27:46; Mk 15:34)

- The message I took in as a child: I realized that if God would "abandon" His Son—His only begotten Son (Jn 3:16), and "Beloved Son, in whom I am [God is] well pleased" (Mt 3:17)—especially when "His Beloved Son" was in sheer agony and in His great time of need—what made me think that God would ever be there for *me*? My younger self reasoned that if God would abandon and not help His very own Son on the crucifix, then I, who God was probably mad at and was not so "beloved" by God, do not stand a chance—*ever*—in both God's eyes and in my own eyes! I felt, in common vernacular, "screwed."

I sobbed. I intuitively knew I had hit subconscious gold. My tears were an indication to me that I had unearthed something significant, and now that it had come to the surface, it was time to clear it and let it go.

Synchronicities

I then experienced an amazing sequence of synchronicities. During this same time period, I was taking some classes at a local Science of Mind / Religious Science church. As fate would have it, two things happened almost simultaneously.

First, I learned about the "metaphysical" (beyond the physical / beyond the literal) interpretation of the Bible. The metaphysical interpretation of Lot's wife turning to salt is this:

- Salt was a preservative used at the time the Bible was written.

- Lot's wife wanted to hold on to her past. She looked backward, not forward.

- One "freezes" and gets stuck by putting one's focus on preserving the past.

I came to believe that the story was an extended metaphor—an allegory—as are most stories in the Bible.

Also, I learned during my metaphysical interpretation of the Bible studies that anytime the words "female" or "woman" are used, or a story of "a woman" is mentioned, these words represent a metaphor regarding one's *emotions*—and do not refer to or apply only to a specific woman or to a specific gender.

The metaphysical interpretation of the story of Lot's wife: Your emotions become stuck when you want to preserve your past by putting attention and focus on it. Looking backward thwarts forward progression. The new lesson, and, as a result, my new intention: Release my past and move forward toward a new and improved future.

The second synchronicity was learning about the Lamsa Bible. George Lamsa, who was born and raised in the same region as Jesus, The Christ, was a native speaker of Aramaic and translated the Bible from the original Aramaic.

Realizing there were some discrepancies between Bible translations, I looked up Bible verses that triggered an intense and deep-seated disturbance and a perceived chasm in my relationship with God. This is one of the aforementioned passages as it appears in the Lamsa Bible (Mt 27:46):

> And about the ninth hour, Jesus cried out with a loud voice and said, Eli, Eli, lemana shabakthani! My God, my God, for this I was spared! [This was my destiny.]

I cried. Jesus was not crying out to God, "Where the heck are you?!" Jesus was actually looking down from the crucifix, trying to comfort those crying and mourning His torture and impending death. He was essentially saying, "Hey, everyone! It's all okay! I was born to do this! It's all going to be okay!"

At that same moment, I realized that it was *me. I* was the one who had held such long-standing beliefs against God. I realized that *I* was actually making judgments against God. *I* was using my negative judgments as my rationale for my separation from God. *I* was the one who was distant and wanting to punish God! *I* was not there—not present—for God; *I* was the one who was withholding in my relationship with God. In all of these judgments, and more, *I was projecting onto God.*

I realized that prior to that moment, all of my life I felt like a "victim" of unrequited love. I thought I was "the giver," "the doer"—experiencing only a one-way relationship. I realized that *I* had never even given God a chance. I only perceived God through the eyes of a scared, confused, and beaten child.

My image of God and my negative emotions toward God were frozen at that time in my life when I was young, vulnerable, hurt (emotionally and physically), and extremely impressionable. It was time to let go of this God, the God of my hurt *inner child.*

With that in mind, I turned to this quote:

> When I was a child, I spoke as a child, I understood as a child, I thought as a child; but when I became a man, I

> put away childish things. For now we see through a mir-
> ror, darkly; but then face-to-face. Now I know in part;
> but then shall I know even as also I am known. And now
> abide faith, hope, love, these three; but the greatest of
> these is love. (Lamsa, 1 Cor 13: 11–13)

Setting my intention to "abide faith, hope, and love," with an emphasis on love—especially as it related to my relationship with God—I pressed on. It was time to release my past misconceptions and misperceptions, discover new ways of thinking and being, and implement them.

Having core issues within my unconscious / subconscious / energy field brought to light by meditation, prayer, and divining (applied kinesiology) and brought to the realm of my conscious-ness, I could release my past and move forward. Fueled by a strong intention to clear / release entrenched negativity and heal, I was able to address the issues that were disturbing my inner peace. With the assistance of God / Spirit / My Highest Power, *plus* with use of some elements of clearing modalities I studied and / or become certified in as a practitioner, I was able to easily clear and release the negative programming within myself.

With Aristotle's quote "Nature abhors a vacuum" in mind, I began to explore what it was I wanted to fill in within the space I had cleared. Through prayer, meditation, self-forgiveness / self-re-leasing work, journaling, and inner dialoguing, I was open and could more clearly attune to inner messages. I asked God / Spirit / My Highest Power / Big Love to reveal Her / His / Its True Nature to me. Here is a brief list of what was revealed:

I Am ...
unwavering and unconditionally:
loving, forgiving, supporting, caring, nurturing, providing, adoring, advocating, cheerleading, supporting.

Chapter 5

Being Humble

On a human level, I will always fall short of the ego's perception of "perfection." I can, however, at all times, in all things, and in all ways strive for personal excellence. On a soul level, God's perfection resides within each and every one of us here and now. I can—at all times, in all things, and in all ways—strive for that Truth to be my reality and my experience.

—Dr. Linda Humphreys

During the discovery of my blocks and my subsequent quest for Truth, another issue—or rather, concept—appeared. When it came forward, I felt it had to be addressed immediately. The concept was "being humble." I intuitively sensed this would be a lynchpin for me in my spiritual rediscovery and "recovery" process.

Merriam-Webster defines humble as "not proud or haughty … ranking low in a hierarchy or scale: insignificant."

I understand and agree that being around a braggart can be challenging. I imagine most other people would feel the same. Having said that, bragging has a totally different and lower vibration / energy than not bragging.

There are people who judge anyone and everyone as "bragging," regardless of where the *other* person is coming from energetically, because of *their own* misperceptions, negative feelings about themselves, and where *they* are coming from. Being around that type of negative and judgmental personality can be equally challenging.

Somewhere along the way, I believe the concept of being humble (humility) has been misinterpreted, misrepresented, distorted, mistaught, and incorrectly preached. Some people believe that if someone is "not humble," that person thinks of himself / herself as being "perfect"—as if these terms were the antithesis of each other.

Having said that, I do *not* believe that God / Spirit / Highest Power wants, expects, demands, or commands us to have any perception of ourselves or feelings of being "insignificant." As a beloved daughter of God, I do *not* believe that I am "ranking low in a hierarchy or scale" or "insignificant."

As a beloved daughter of God / Spirit / Highest Power, I do believe in striving for personal excellence—not perfection—because the pursuit of perfection is a construct of one's ego. Also, as a beloved daughter of God / Spirit / Highest Power, I do believe that within everyone is an aspect of the perfection of God: one's soul.

—Dr. Linda Humphreys

Here is how I make the distinction between bragging and being humble:

- Bragging: If I believe I accomplished something all by myself and without the assistance of God / Spirit / Highest Power (and perhaps others), I believe that type of energy, attitude, thinking, and personality is centered more within my own ego.

- Being humble: If I believe I accomplished something by being supported and assisted by God / Spirit / Highest Power (and perhaps others), I believe that type of energy, attitude, thinking, and personality is centered outside my ego.

The sharing of a personal "victory," if a person shares with energy that is coming from their heart and not coming from their ego, is a delight to hear from others—and a delight for others to hear as well—especially if all parties are expressing and listening from a heart- and soul-centered place. If, however, a listener is not listening from a heart- and soul-centered place, anything said by another—even the expression of someone who is coming from a heart- and soul-centered place—can be misconstrued, misinterpreted, and judged by the listener. The second listener's perceptual filter is rooted in a hurting, lacking, less than, judgmental, inferior (yet at the same time superior, because all judgments are rooted in the energy of superiority), and their own ego place. I believe it is important not to take in another's negative reaction—which is coming from their own false sense and misinterpretation of what it means to be truly humble. This type of listener's negative reactions are coming from their own negativity, judgments, and ego.

What Is God's Definition of Being Humble?

While meditating about the concept of being humble, I asked God for God's definition of the concept. During the meditation, I felt tears stream down my face as emotions welled up from deep within. I experienced what I call an "Aha! Awe" moment. Here is what I gleaned from my experience.

Being Humble = Experiencing Awe—and Awe Leads to Gratitude

I experienced profound awe regarding God. I experienced the greatness, power, majesty, perfection, and love of God, and it was all so much bigger and much more grand than I am. It was overwhelming, staggering, and breathtaking. Just the mere thought of my experience stirs a profound sense of gratitude within me.

I experienced a profound sense of God not only surrounding me, but actually connecting *with* me. I experienced no separation from God. I experienced what has been called "The Oneness" between God and my soul, God as my soul and the soul of everyone and everything. When I recall my experience, the words that come to mind to describe it are *profound*, *breathtaking*, *inspiring*, *blissful*, *awe-producing*, and *awesome*. All of these contributed to a profound sense of gratitude.

I experienced what I believe is God's definition of being humble. God, as True, Unconditional Love, never diminishes us and never wants or demands us to have any feelings of being "insignificant." I also believe that Heavenly Mother / Father God would not want us, as their beloved daughters and sons, to perceive ourselves as inferior or low in importance, quality, or hierarchy in any way, shape, or form.

I experienced God as majestic, the Source of all that is good. To me, that is what God is—and so much more. That thought inspires a breathtaking awe from deep within me. At the same time, I did not experience any sense of separation, inferiority, lowliness, and so on. I experienced awe, wonder, and gratitude in and for the grandeur of God / Spirit / Highest Power.

I also experienced a sense of relief and release, as the pressure was finally off. I understood that *I* was not actually responsible for the universe. (Funny to say, but true.) There was something above and beyond me that I was connected with and was within me, within everyone, and within everything. There was no sense of separation and diminishment in any way. There was only enhancement, upliftment, and connection.

Being Humble = The Willingness to Step Out of Your Own Way

During this meditation, I realized that humility / being humble is actually the willingness to step out of my own way. It involves setting aside what my thinking mind judges as true and how it reacts via defining, compartmentalizing, and labeling things. Additionally, it means setting aside what the thinking mind deems as the best way to react and behave—say and do. It involves having the willingness to:

- Take a moment and breathe,

- Suspend the thinking mind and its reactive response mechanisms,

- Connect to Spirit Within, and

- Come from a more loving / heart- and soul-centered place prior to and during any action / reaction.

Being Humble = Openness and Receptivity to God / Spirit / Highest Power

I also realized that after I step out of my own way and make a conscious connection to Spirit Within, I experience a state of openness and receptivity to more loving, inner peace, guidance, synchronicities, and wondrous adventures. I could go on and on as there is no limit to what is available when one is open and receptive to connecting to The Oneness of Spirit.

Being Humble = Connecting to Love / God Within and Throughout

By being more connected to The Oneness of Spirit, it connects me to Love / God Within my own being. It also connects me to Love / God Within others—and in all things. It takes me out of my thinking / ego mind and reactivity and puts me in a more loving, heart- and soul-centered and peaceful state of being.

Being Humble = Not My—but Thy Will Be Done

As I followed these steps in my conscious mind, I realized there was a better way of being than letting my own thinking mind rule and guide me. This requires surrendering—availing myself to Spirit and the willingness to surrender to a more loving way of being. It involved a relinquishing of "my will be done" to "Thy Will be done"—to truly surrender by yielding my self / my thinking mind / ego and being open to allow for the expression of Spirit.

Being Humble = Relaxing and Releasing = True Surrendering

By setting my own reactive, thinking mind and will aside, and by releasing mind-conceived, will-filled expectations, I can relax. I can breathe. I know that all will unfold exactly as it should. I am cared for and taken care of. God is in charge. I simply need to be willing and open to being guided and led by God Within and Throughout. All is well. All will be well. I don't need to "do," "fix," or control anything and / or anyone. I can let go and surrender my tightfisted reins. This is True surrender.

Being Humble in Action = Alignment + Service + Gratitude

When I find myself in alignment in this way, I truly experience this:

I *Am* God's hands and feet.

Perhaps even more accurately stated:

I *Am* God's hands and feet, mind, and heart.

and …

I *Am* grateful!

These statements embody True humility—stepping out of my own way—by being open, willing, and receptive, availing myself to God, aligning myself with God Within and Throughout, and by serving others (and in turn, myself) with gratitude.

By surrendering the reactive response of the thinking mind (which triggers habitual, reactive thoughts, behaviors, and emotions, plus physiological response mechanisms), the door opens for greater conscious connection and the experience of The Oneness. I believe, more accurately, it reflects the experience of what I received as God's definition of humility—and it is *AWE*some!

I have come to believe that True humility is intended to inspire, not diminish anyone in any way. It is an experience of being in awe of the Divine. It is intended to serve as a call to set our ego (with its thinking mind and judgments) aside—to step forward and connect with something much greater and more grand within ourselves.

True humility is a state of conscious connection—a union—of the Divine Throughout with the Divine Within. It is an experience of no separation, of openness and receptivity, and of the willingness to surrender to a more loving way. It is the yielding of the thinking mind's reactive and judgmental nature to a conscious connection with Love. It is an experience of Thy Will—and not my ego's will—being done, of being in the flow—an experience of The Oneness. It is an experience of Loving. It is an experience of God.

—Dr. Linda Humphreys

Chapter 6

Grace

My new definition of **GRACE:** *God's Resources Activated Connecting Everyone and Everything. It is inside of each and every one of us 24/7/365. We can consciously activate it to connect to the Divine Within. This also is the catalyst to connections to the Divine Throughout—creating synchronicities and miracles.*

—*Dr. Linda Humphreys*

Another concept used in religious contexts, and one which was a source of a lot of confusion for me, is *grace*. I am not referring to "saying grace" as in expressing gratitude for meals prior to eating. I am referring to the concept of *grace* as referred to in expressions such as "begging for God's grace," "There but for the grace of God go I," and so on.

According to *Baltimore Catechism*, there are different kinds of grace:

55. How many kinds of grace are there?
There are two kinds of grace: sanctifying grace and actual grace.

56. What does sanctifying grace do for us?
Sanctifying grace:

> *first,* makes us holy and pleasing to God;

> *second,* makes us adopted children of God;

> *third,* makes us temples of the Holy Ghost;

> *fourth,* gives us the right to heaven.

57. What is actual grace?
Actual grace is a supernatural help of God which enlightens our mind and strengthens our will to do good and to avoid evil.

58. What are the principal ways of obtaining grace?
The principal ways of obtaining grace are prayer and the sacraments, especially the Holy Eucharist.

After re-reading this, I can understand where some of my confusion and frustration about trying to "figure out" grace stemmed from. These types of answers—especially in books that were intended for children—seem very "head-y." Reading these answers tied my "monkey mind" (my busy ego mind) into knots!

As a child and until I recently went within to explore the concept, I always thought of grace as something that was magically bestowed on *some* people—occasionally, sporadically, unpredictably, and randomly. It felt as if "earning" or "deserving" grace was a crap shoot. It was something to beg, beseech, and implore God for. It seemed as if acquiring it was an elusive formula that I could not decipher or figure out—at least that's what it was for me.

I decided to go within and ask God what God's definition of grace was. This is what came forward:

Grace = God's Loving Energy

- Grace is within each and every one of us.

- It is *always* present—and always has been present.

- It never diminishes, waivers, wanes, ebbs, or lessens.

- Grace is the catalyst of synchronicities and being "in the flow."

- It can also be thought of as an opening—a channel that connects us to the Divine—both Within and Throughout.

- You can put conscious and direct focus on the opening of your heart / God Mind, which activates Grace Within to connect with Grace Throughout.

I asked what the energetic qualities of grace were. This is what was revealed:

- Willingness to surrender
- Surrender / Humility (see Chapter 5)
- Open expectancy of love, joy, synchronicities, miracles
- Deep knowing that all is being divinely orchestrated
- Inner peace because of the deep knowing
- Always available connection to The Oneness

My playful *inner child* asked for an acronym for God's concept of grace. Much to my delight, this is what came forward:

- **G**od's
- **R**esources
- **A**ctivated
- **C**onnecting
- **E**veryone and everything

Images of Grace

I asked for images of grace. This is what was revealed to me:

- *Grace is akin to a blessed oil that facilitates a smooth, unencumbered, flow of energy—and energy in action.*
- *The Source of Grace—this blessed oil well—is both God Within and God Throughout. When in alignment, we are "in the zone." Grace helps facilitate this alignment. Grace is the alignment.*

- *We are like an electric plug-in socket for grace. Both the plug and the cord connecting us to God are within. This plugged-in energy connection with God Within is grace.*

- *God / Spirit / Highest Power is the main "power line." Like electricity, it is always present and readily available. We merely have to flip the power switch / God's Light switch on. We are the ones that control the "dimmer" dial.*

- *Grace is an unobstructed and doorless portal within. It is actually like a portal-less portal because there is no confinement of entry. The portal is grace. There is no need to knock, no block and no lock on grace. When you go within, you are in grace. (Even when you do not go within, grace is ever-present.) Grace is always open—always there. Waiting for you ...*

- *There are those who have allowed themselves—and have allowed others—to put much in front of grace. They think that the portal is obstructed. Some allow this perceived / misperceived obstruction to appear as "real." There could be nothing further from the Truth. The Truth is that there is no separation between you and grace.*

- *Grace is also the hand of God always reaching out to you; the loving embrace of God always longing to cradle you; it is the heart of God always loving you. Grace is you—as you are created and meant to be—and can be if you so allow.*

And so it is.

Grace is always present. We simply need to consciously and intentionally plug into it and make that connection. Additionally, we are also meant to be energy receptacles for Grace Throughout. Combined, we truly do become God's hands and feet on Earth.

> Grace is the embodiment of God's love. Grace is God's love in action. Grace is God's love made manifest through us and to us. Grace is God's love within and throughout everyone and everything.
>
> —Dr. Linda Humphreys

Another image was that of a sky filled with billowy dark clouds—and rays of sunshine piercing through the clouds' thick layers, illuminating places where the beams land. (The appearance of the beams of light kept alternating between actual beams and golden cords connecting us—bridging us—with the Divine.)

Though I may not see the sunshine, the sun is forever shining—whether I remember that concept or whether I forget. The sun and its illuminations are omnipresent in the universe. So is God—whether I remember it or whether I forget. This image is also a visual metaphor for how I view Grace Throughout.

Combining the visual metaphors of the energetic electric plug-in socket and the ever-shining sun breaking through dark clouds, the visual of the sun beams radiating down can be thought of as a representation of an energetic extension cord to the ever-present Divine Throughout. If we plug into it, that energetic cord will connect us to the ever-radiating love of God—both Within and Throughout.

My energetic impression regarding grace was that if there is some kind of "effort-ing" involved—it *is God's effort-ing to reach out to us, to beckon us to connect with God's Heart Within and Throughout!* It is our task to allow for grace, accept grace, own grace, and *be* grace.

> When I am plugged in to both Grace Within and Grace Throughout, miracles happen and synchronicities abound. I am in the flow and am one with the Divine.
>
> —Dr. Linda Humphreys

Additional insights:

- Grace is for everyone.

- Grace is in everyone.

- You are walking channels of grace.

- Grace was never meant to be taught or viewed:
  - *as a selective gift bestowed on a few select people,*
  - *as something that needs to be earned,*
  - *as something we need to deserve, or*
  - *as something you are ever without.*

- You are an embodiment of love and grace.

- Just as you are love—you are grace.

- And so it always was.

- And so it always shall be.

The **GRACE** of God (**G**od's **R**esources **A**ctivated **C**onnecting **E**veryone and Everything) begets even more **GRACE** (**G**od's **R**eality **A**ctivated and **C**onsciously **E**nergized).

—Dr. Linda Humphreys

Chapter 7

God Adores You

Just as a baby does not need to do anything to earn the love of its parents, you don't need to do anything to earn God's adoration. God adores you. There is not anything you could do to diminish, deter, nor cease God from adoring you. God adores you. No matter how you feel, what you think, believe, or were told or taught—GOD ADORES YOU! God simply and utterly adores you exactly as you are today—this moment and every moment of your life.

—Dr. Linda Humphreys

God loves you. Even better stated, God *adores* you. That's right—*you*!

God adores me too! God adores everyone. That's right—*everyone*! God adores the other sports team you want to defeat, the person you are judging and withholding your love and forgiveness from, the person or group's sexual preferences and / or nature you judge as wrong / bad / sinful, the person who disagrees with your politics, the political leaders you judge as evil / wrong / bad. God adores everyone. There are no exceptions. Period.

As I define it, adoring love invokes a quality of devotion. Adoration infuses love and embodies these energetic qualities (just to name a few):

- Sacred
- Earnest
- Infinite
- Constant

- Unconditional

- Unrelenting

- Unwavering

- Omnipresent

- Expansive

- Uplifting

Another way of thinking about this: God = Adoring Love.

***

Adoring Love is who God is. Adoring Love is what God does. Adoring Love is God's specialty. As Adoring Love, there is no space for judgment, condemnation, ridicule, separation, damnation, ill will, ill thoughts, or other "ill" things.

God simply and utterly adores you—through and through, head to toe, body and soul. After all, God created you. You are God's pride and joy, delight, beloved daughter / beloved son. You are God's masterpiece—exactly as you are today. God adores you— always has, always will. God adores you in all ways—always.

God is your DNA: Divine Nature Always.

—Dr. Linda Humphreys

You are soul—a divine spirit. God is your spiritual Mother and Father. God is your DNA: Divine Nature Always. All you have to do is align and activate with your True spiritual DNA. Once this occurs, miracles happen. Actually, simply having that divine shift in perception is a miracle, as A Course in Miracles states.

Regardless of how you feel at any given moment, the Truth of who you really are will always remain an unwavering Truth—forever and ever—no matter how much you try to reason it away or figure it out and deem it contrary to your thinking ego / personality mind; regardless of whether you choose to accept, believe, or deny this Truth. Additionally, regardless of what others tell or have told you or have preached to you as contradictory to this Truth, it will always be the Truth.

> Give your "monkey mind" a hiatus—a much-needed R&R—relaxation and restoration—to align with your spiritual DNA: Divine Nature Always.
> —Dr. Linda Humphreys

God holds the vision of who and what you truly are: God's beloved daughter / beloved son. The origin of the word *sin* has ties to archery—and not to hell and eternal damnation as it is preached today. Even when we "sin" and "miss the mark" by making unloving choices and do unloving things, God cherishes and adores us—always and forever.

As we learn in *A Course in Miracles*, every moment is a moment to choose again. God is so gracious and loving that God provides us with many moments in which to choose again, filled with way-showers, teachers, guides, lessons, inner guidance, and synchronicities—just to name a few—to help guide us back to a conscious connection to God and our Authentic Self—our heart and soul—and to the hearts and souls of others.

This, and more, has been revealed to me through meditation, inner inquiring, epiphanies, and through an abundance of inspirations. This, and more, is what I am now *experiencing* as a result of my "GOD Project."

I hold these Truths for you—as dearly as I hold them for myself. This work is not for wussies. I invite you to take the very brave and courageous step of exploring, with the intention of ultimately revealing, who you truly are by doing your own "GOD Project."

Chapter 8

Owning Your Divinity

I believe that owning your connection with God / Spirit / Highest Power—The Divine Within—and owning your Inner Divinity (which serves to activate your Spiritual DNA—Divine Nature Always) are key to experiencing inner healing, transformation, and miracles.

—*Dr. Linda Humphreys*

I believe that regardless of the issue, another element is imperative for True transformation to take place. That element is *ownership*.

Too often, ownership of our True relationship position, especially in terms of our relationship with God, is skewed. This misperception, I believe, is extraordinarily detrimental on multiple levels. While I believe God is Supreme, and I will never have equal footing or position within the realm of the Supreme, there is a perspective that is more aligned with the Truth than what we have been taught and what, too often, is still being promulgated and propagated. Believing we are to perceive ourselves as *worms* and that God perceives us as such is inaccurate and totally incongruent to who we truly are and to God's True Nature.

It would not be even in the realm of possibility for God / Spirit / Highest Power to entertain such a notion, vibration, or perception unless God was to turn against God's own True Nature. After clearing blocks and imbalances, setting my intention to experience the True Nature of God, and finally knowing and experiencing "God is Love / God as Love," I turned my attention to discovering what my own (and every human's) True nature actually is.

Our True Nature

I believe that *original sin* (and again, defining *sin* as an archery term meaning *to miss the mark*) is actually about forgetting the True Nature of God. Additionally, it is our forgetting the True Nature of our Inner Divinity. We are "in sin" when we do not acknowledge, live, create with, accept, embrace, act, see, and call upon our own *Original Innocence*—an aspect of our Inner Divinity—and everyone else's as well. If we are not unconditionally loving—as our "Mother / Father" God / Spirit / Highest Power is, created us to be, and even *commands* us to be—we truly are *sinning* by "missing the mark."

When Jesus was about to be stoned to death, He pointed out to those that opposed Him that He had performed many good works, which stemmed from God. He asked them which one of His good works they wanted to stone Him for.

> "We are not stoning you for any good work," they replied, "but for blasphemy, because you, a mere man, claim to be God."
>
> Jesus answered them, "Is it not written in your Law, 'I have said you are gods'?" (Jn 10:33-34 NIV)

We must learn to acknowledge, own, and activate our Inner Divinity. We must encourage and support others in acknowledging and embracing their own Inner Divinity too. Again, I believe we truly "sin"—miss the mark—if we continue, both consciously and subconsciously, to ignore, diminish, and negate this Truth. We must embrace, embody, and infuse our entire being with the light of this Holy Truth: We *are* beloved daughters and sons of the Most High.

Perhaps as your ego / personality / "small" self you believe you cannot do / be / have whatever may come to mind for you. However, when you are consciously connected to your Inner Divinity, anything can be accomplished.

Accepting anything less than the Truth of your *Original Innocence* and this "original immaculate conception" of yourself is merely an excuse for not living up to who and what you Truly are and fulfilling your True potential. Believing you are lowly and a victim (as in "Who am I to do / be / have ...? I could never do / be / have..."—with a "poor me" attitude) while being passive and pessimistic (as in "What's the use? I can't ...!"—with an "Eeyore" attitude) perpetuates a concocted story that you either created or took on from others. Time to release and let that victim story and attitude go!

I saw a bumper sticker that read: "God Doesn't Make Junk!" I agree with that sentiment. I also believe that God certainly did not make us *worms*. As a beloved daughter of the Most High, nothing *worm*-like is in my spiritual DNA. I also affirm and embrace this same Truth about everyone.

God's spiritual DNA is in Jesus, in me, and in everyone on the planet. We are all cut from the same cloth.

Prior to a meditation and with the intention of owning and anchoring the energy that I am a beloved daughter of God, I requested that a new mantra come into my awareness. This is what I was gifted with:

"I Am a beloved daughter of God, in whom God is well pleased!"

To this day, it is one of my most favorite mantras.

Believing that the soul is an aspect of God, I believe each of us holds an aspect of God Within. I believe that God is Sovereign and "King of Kings" and I am a beloved daughter of God. That makes me, at the very least, a spiritual princess, right?

—Dr. Linda Humphreys

I do not believe it is wrong to stand up, own, and share about my strived-for positive accomplishments, as I believe all of my "victories" are God-originated, inspired, infused, aligned, and guided.

One of my favorite quotes was, I believe, "channeled" by God / Spirit / Highest Power through Marianne Williamson in her seminal book, *A Return to Love*:

> Our deepest fear is not that we are inadequate. Our deepest fear is that we are powerful beyond measure. It is our light, not our darkness that most frightens us. We ask ourselves, Who am I to be brilliant, gorgeous, talented, fabulous? Actually, who are you *not* to be? You are a child of God. Your playing small does not serve the world. There is nothing enlightened about shrinking so that other people won't feel insecure around you. We are all meant to shine, as children do. We were born to make manifest the glory of God that is within us. It's not just in some of us; it's in everyone. And as we let our own light shine, we unconsciously give other people permission to do the same. As we are liberated from our own fear, our presence automatically liberates others.

To this day, this quote inspires, delights, and informs some of my thoughts, actions, and, most definitely, meditations. These words have truly become words to live by.

Chapter 9

Self-Love and Loving Others

Loving others without loving yourself is akin to exhaling without breathing in. Your life-force energy cannot be sustained in this manner.

—Dr. Linda Humphreys

In addition to observing clients' challenges in their relationships with God, I have noticed the same people have challenges with their relationships with themselves. I believe they stem, like my own challenges did, from religious indoctrination and dogma.

The Importance of Self-Love

Loving oneself is not taught. In fact, I believe that loving one's self is discouraged because it is considered not being "humble" in the traditional religious context. When judged in that context, I have heard self-love described by others as "egocentric," "a vice," "an insult to God," and "a sin."

An illustration of the importance of self-love can be witnessed every time one flies on an airplane. Before the beginning of each flight, the flight attendant says a variation of this:

> In case of emergency, oxygen masks will drop down in front of you. Please pull the mask down toward your face and place the mask over your mouth and nose. If you are traveling with a child, please attend to yourself first, then the child. Breathe normally. Adjust the headband to suit yourself.

There you have it: self-care, self-regard, and self-love in action. Even the airlines realize that you are useless in the care of others if you don't first care for yourself.

I have found spiritual and life messages in that announcement. The announcement clearly states—even requests:

- "Please attend to yourself first."
  Lesson: First and foremost, take care of yourself. Please.

- "Breathe normally."
  Lesson: Taking care of yourself should be normal and natural. As normal and natural as breathing normally.

- "Adjust the headband to suit yourself."
  Lesson: Be comfortable; find comfort; make adjustments. This will support you in taking care of yourself and in taking care of others in turn.

I strongly believe that for any relationship to be perceived as satisfying, healthy, supportive, and balanced, all parties must be fully present, engaged in their loving, and capable of giving as well as receiving. I also believe that we must love ourselves to fully and completely love God and others.

—Dr. Linda Humphreys

A Truly Loving Person ... or One-Way Victim?

Another client observation is that these same people tend to view themselves as "victims" of others, life, and God. They perceive themselves as someone things are done "to." I use the term "one-way victim" in referring to this type of perceptual tendency.

When someone is in the low vibration of "victimhood," that energy spills into each and every relationship that person has. It becomes a lens through which he or she perceives all relationships. The use of the lens of victimhood can be habitually ingrained and sustained, and can become an entrenched aspect of someone's personality.

In my opinion, those who carry the dense vibration of "victim / victimhood" are not passive aggressive. I believe they are actively aggressive; there is nothing passive about making sure they maintain their delusion that in each and every situation and relationship, something was done *to* them. Viewing life through this lens allows "victims" to relinquish their personal responsibility for their actions, reactions, attitudes, and so forth. Sustaining that illusion requires a lot of energy and effort!

We cannot remain "one-way victims." We need to balance loving God, ourselves, and others to experience the totality that love has to offer.

If we have blocks and barriers toward perceiving and thus truly receiving God's love, how could we possibly truly love God? Ourselves? Others?

—Dr. Linda Humphreys

The Importance of Loving Others

Going within again, I asked myself, Do I truly understand the depth and breadth of God's love for me? If it is being given unconditionally and unwavering—24 / 7 / 365—what percentage am I truly tuned into 24 / 7 / 365? What percentage am I perceiving? Owning? Extending to others?

Love God *and* My Neighbor …
The Way I Love *Myself*?

Jesus was challenged by "scholars of religious law" and asked, of all of the commandments, which *one* was the greatest.

> Jesus replied, "The most important commandment is this: Listen, O Israel! The LORD our God is the one and only LORD. And you must love the LORD your God with all your heart, all your soul, all your mind, and all your strength.'" (Mark 12:29-30 NLT)

Without missing a beat, Jesus added:

> The second is equally important: "'Love your neighbor as yourself.' No other commandment is greater than these." (Mark 12:31 NLT)

Jesus entwined the *equal importance* of loving God and one's "neighbor." He made no separation, no distinction between the importance of loving God and loving others—because loving others is an act of loving God. Jesus did not separate the loving of God from the loving of others.

Additionally, the emphasis of loving one's neighbor "as yourself" stresses the importance of self-love. Another way of approaching and thinking about self-love is this: The type of love (quality and quantity) you are giving yourself is the type of love you are giving others.

Questions to consider:

- What is the quality and quantity of self-love you are experiencing?

- What is the quality and quantity of love you are expressing?

- How would you imagine others would describe the quality and quantity of loving they are receiving from you?

The concept of loving others is so vital that Jesus issued the following commandment:

> This is my commandment: Love each other in the same way I have loved you. (John 15:12 NLT)

The Interconnected and Inner Connected Nature of Loving

During a mediation, my query was as follows: Why are we witnessing widespread hate crimes, violence against others, rudeness, incivility, disregard, and lack of compassion toward others, just to name a few? What came forward for me was how interconnected loving God, loving oneself, and loving others is. During a meditation, I received a vision of a trinity that looked similar to one of the *Baltimore Catechism* illustrations I grew up with. However, this trinity was comprised of the following aspects: loving God, loving myself, and loving others.

As simple and as, perhaps, repetitive and / or familiar it may seem, the experience of this vision had a profound effect on me. Shortly after the meditation, I came upon a quote from the New Testament. To me, the quote demonstrates a perfect verbalization of the vision I experienced—and it was verbalized by Jesus, The Christ.

> I have loved you even as the Father has loved me. Remain in my love. (John 15:9 NLT)

> If we are "commanded" to love God and to love others "as yourself," and if we lack self-love, how could we possibly truly love God and love others? We have to remove any and all blocks and barriers to loving everyone with all of our hearts, souls, minds, and strength—including ourselves.
>
> —Dr. Linda Humphreys

Chapter 10

The Fallacy of Unrequited Love

Until we have clarity about what self-love actually is, why it is vital, and how it is acquired and mastered, we will continue to perceive ourselves as "victims"—reinforcing the perspective of "unrequited love." The fallacy of "victim" / "unrequited love" affects every relationship in our lives—including our perceived relationship with God.

—Dr. Linda Humphreys

Believing that you perceive what you believe and believe what you perceive, you reap what you sow, and what you give, you get, I decided to look within to see what I was believing, perceiving, sowing, and giving.

I wanted to disconnect from the lower vibration of victim / victimhood, so I had to go within and unplug from any and all false beliefs about my love to God being unilateral, one-way, and unrequited. I also had to unplug from any and all false beliefs about God's love for me.

I have come to realize that it was actually God who got the short straw in our relationship. If there was a one-way direction of loving, it was—and always has been—from God to me. I was the absentee party in our relationship.

—Dr. Linda Humphreys

Realizing how interconnected my perception of God, self-love, and loving others was and how off-base I was about all of it, I also examined my misperceptions regarding the universe.

> Ours is not an "unrequited" universe. There is always give and take, back and forth, ebb and flow. I believe the feeling of unrequited love is impossible as it relates to God. Any semblance of victimhood or unidirectional loving within our consciousness / subconscious / energy field must be addressed and removed for us to have a more direct, intimate, and loving experience of and relationship with God.
>
> —Dr. Linda Humphreys

I now know that loving oneself is an expression of loving God. Additionally, loving oneself and loving God brings more loving to others—and ultimately—to the planet. Given the current state of political and civil unrest, upset, anger, and dissonance, I believe it is imperative to come into alignment with our True Selves and God's True Nature—now more than ever.

It is time to take proactive measures to clear out inner negativity, disharmony, grudges, resentments, disturbances, judgments, anger, and any sense of being a victim. Additionally—and equally important—it is imperative to remove any and all blocks to being more loving and experiencing more loving toward yourself, others—and to the Source of Love: GOD.

We need to shed the cloak of victimhood as it relates to all relationships—including our perceived relationship with God. Doing so will allow us to have a full, rich, and intimate experience of God's loving—and of the universe—as being a more loving place.

—Dr. Linda Humphreys

Chapter 11

Why GETTING GOD Is Imperative

I believe the challenge of our perception—and misperception—of our relationship with God is both universal and pandemic. This disconnection with the Divine contributes to dissonance and discord on the planet. As such, this requires immediate attention and healing.

—Dr. Linda Humphreys

I have experienced everything written in this book on visceral, spiritual, psychological, mental, emotional, and energetic levels. As you are reading this book, you may discover that while my religious indoctrination and media influences were different from what you were exposed to, you are still left with the same emotions: You sense something is missing, feel distance between you and God, and want to experience a more personal, intimate, and loving experience of God.

You Are Not Alone

I live and work in an extremely diverse community. A myriad of religions is practiced, people of different races mingle, and a great mixture of cultural offerings surround me on a daily basis. I am blessed to have the opportunity to partake in the mix of it all—especially the variety of eclectic, spiritually related services, venues, and offerings.

Based on the conversations I have had with others during coaching, metaphysical counseling, and energy-work practitioner sessions, I realize that an individual's perceived "lack of a loving relationship with a loving God" is extremely common, as well as perplexing—and a source of great anxiety, stress, confusion, and frustration. I have also witnessed within others the same kind of fear of God and distancing placed between themselves and God that I once experienced.

I have discovered that my experience of formerly perceiving God as separate and apart from me is not a singular experience. Others have confessed and expressed to me that they perceive their relationship with God as strained, frustrating, perplexing, tentative, distant, and more.

Making Your Intention Your Reality

More than anything, I have found that the common themes, both in myself and in others, are the desire for greater inner peace and for the intimate experience of Divine Love. With the strong intention of experiencing more of those elements, both within and throughout your life, coupled with a willingness to explore, clear, and release whatever conscious and unconscious blocks and energetic imbalances exist, your heartfelt intention can become an inner reality.

When you clear and release conscious or subconscious energetic blocks from your energy field—blocks you have held and carried for many years—you can then be a more open and receptive channel for the flow of God's love. To experience that, I believe, is truly "heaven on Earth."

We could certainly use a lot more of it at this time, wouldn't you agree?

While my struggles, challenges, and misperceptions surrounding my understanding of and my relationship with God may have unique elements (just as everyone's does), I believe the challenge is common. The explosive proliferation of haters, chaos, suicides, violence, and any and all types of separation and against-ness are proof that we need to be GETTING GOD—on all levels ... now!

—Dr. Linda Humphreys

Chapter 12

Analogies of Transformation

If it were not for the caterpillar acquiescing to its True nature and immersing itself deeply within its own cocoon, the transformation to a butterfly would never occur.

—Dr. Linda Humphreys

There are two beautiful and fitting illustrations or analogies that exemplify what doing clearing and release work on metaphysical energy blocks and imbalances is like. The first is the following quote:

I saw the angel in the marble and carved until
I set him free.   —Michelangelo

This quote is so fitting because the work is akin to carving (or chipping away) calcified, hardened, entrenched core beliefs, images, misperceptions, and judgments of all you are not—to reveal the Truth and beauty of who you truly are both within and throughout, to create inside-out transformation.

Just as Michelangelo chipped away at the marble to release and reveal the angel within the stone, thereby transforming a marble slab into a breathtakingly beautiful work of art, we must do our own chipping away of any and all barriers separating us from experiencing ourselves and others as angels. We must chip away our misperceptions and erroneous conscious and subconscious beliefs. We must chip away any and all doubt of our True nature. We must accept and believe that an angel resides within each and every one of us—and set it free.

—Dr. Linda Humphreys

Additionally, the Rumi quote used in the Introduction is worth revisiting:

> Your task is not to seek for love,
> but merely to seek and find all the barriers
> within yourself that you have built against it.

The other analogy for this type of work is "The Golden Buddha" story. More than 300 years ago, Thailand (known at that time as Siam) was being invaded by the Burmese army. A group of Siamese monks were the guardians of a solid gold statue of Buddha, weighing over 2.5 tons and measuring over ten feet tall. In an effort to protect the statue, they covered the statue with mounds of clay with hopes that the Burmese troops would bypass it and think it was just a worthless lump of clay. The monks were tragically killed, and with them, the secret of where the Golden Buddha lay.

In the 1950s, the monastery was supposed to be relocated. During the excavation process, one of the monks made a discovery through a crack in the clay. He took a flashlight to peer through the crack. The monk saw something shine brightly from within. He gathered the monks together, and they slowly and methodically removed the accumulated clay from the mound, which was approximately one foot in depth. Their patient and meticulous efforts paid off, as underneath the mound of clay was The Golden Buddha. This Golden Buddha is now located in Bangkok, Thailand in the Temple of the Golden Buddha.

Just like the monks in the story above, I believe that our misunderstandings, negativity, judgments, prejudices—and any and all other negative types of energy—need to be and can be washed away. This story is also a wonderful metaphor about the "dirt" we have placed upon our God figure—keeping the True Nature of God obscured. With some tender loving care, God's True Nature can be revealed. I believe that persistent and laser-focused attention, along with gentle and meticulous care, must be applied toward the clearing and releasing of any and all debris that separates us from the shining gold that lies within each and every one of us.

Chapter 13

Our Multiple Minds

There is nothing either good or bad, but thinking makes it so.
—William Shakespeare

Philosopher and Jesuit priest Pierre Teilhard de Chardin said, "We are not human beings having a spiritual experience. We are spiritual beings having a human experience." As such, I believe we have multiple minds:

- The Conscious / Thinking Mind,

- The Unconscious / Subconscious Mind,

- The "Busy" / Ego Mind, and

- The Mind of Consciousness—the God / Spirit / Highest Power Mind.

The Conscious / Thinking Mind

For as long as I can remember, I was taught that we use approximately 10 percent of our brain. Some people call this part of the brain we use the "conscious mind" or the "thinking mind," often using the terms interchangeably. In high school biology, I learned that this mind reasoned, formed cognitive links, processed language, thoughts, created its own logic, and so on.

While all of this may be arguable and highly unscientific in nature, I am simply sharing with you what is commonly taught and espoused.

The Unconscious / Subconscious Mind

The part of your mind that controls autonomic body functions is the unconscious / subconscious mind, which regulates inhaling and exhaling, swallowing, blinking, and so on. This is also the mind that Dr. Joe Dispenza, author and lecturer in the fields of neuroscience and human potential, addresses in his book *Breaking the Habit of Being Yourself.* In it Dr. Dispenza asserts that by the time we are thirty-five years old, 95 percent of who we are—meaning all identifications, both positive and negative associations that lead to behaviors and habits—reside in the subconscious mind.

That made me wonder if when we become thirty-five years old, does some of what was operating in the conscious mind take up residence in the unconscious / subconscious mind? If so, and if 95 percent of what I say, do, and think is not conscious, I wondered, *What is "running the show"?* More specifically, I wondered what was running *my* show? The answer according to Dr. Dispenza (and verifiable by my own experiences): past judgments, old beliefs, habits, rote responses—and other unconscious reactions.

Since the unconscious / subconscious mind does things like "connect the dots" (meaning it relates current experiences to past experiences, reactions, behaviors, perceptions, judgments, beliefs, and so on), we essentially function on autopilot. This means, however, that you (you in the present moment) are not the "pilot." Your past experiences, reactions, behaviors, perceptions, judgments, beliefs, and so on become the pilot. That is "who" and "what" is "running the show."

If you let your life continue on this path, it can become rote, predictable, dull, and frustrating because your responses and reactions are now an engrained, reactive habit. This can lead to "same ol' same ol'"—because regardless of the stimuli, a habit of misperceiving, judging people, places, and things becomes entrenched and engrained—and so do your reactions and responses. As I have heard among support group circles and in other places: "Nothing changes if nothing changes."

The "Busy" / Ego Mind

The "busy mind" is actually a euphemism for what I actually call my "monkey mind." (I also refer to it as my "munching mind," because, like a dog, it wants something to munch or gnaw on.) This is the "mind" that runs the chatter in my head. It is where my "sh@#!y committee" has taken residence and runs with unbridled negativity.

Quite often, I have experienced, observed, and have caught myself immersed in this mind. I have noticed that its chatter runs rampant and unconsciously until it is brought into my awareness. Though awareness does, at times, momentarily suspend its activity, I have found the "busy mind's" babble slips into my unconscious mind where it continues its rant—and triggers subsequent and corresponding reactions. This mind has nothing to do with any type of reason. It simply likes to prattle on and on.

I have also observed that this is the ego's mind. It tends to reflect the reactionary, younger aspect within ourselves (*inner child's* mind). It assesses "threats" by making judgments, reacts in defensive and fear-based ways, and will do anything and everything in its power to simply … survive.

The Mind of Consciousness— The God/Spirit/Highest Power Mind

This is what I believe: As a beloved child of God, with the same spiritual DNA or blueprint as God, we also have a "God Mind."

When I connect with and invoke my God Mind, I am "in the flow." I experience greater intuition, more synchronicities, and The Oneness. I am more loving—and I perceive a greater sense of loving. This is where the magic happens.

—Dr. Linda Humphreys

Another way of describing the "God Mind" is having conscious awareness and connection with soul: your soul, the soul of God, and the soul of others. It is the mind that resides within each and every one of us. It is the mind that we are meant to use and rely upon. Though it may not be the go-to mind that we habitually use, with intention, patience, and practice, one's God Mind can become the predominate mind, force, and influence in our lives—and in the lives of others.

Your soul is not just meant to "sit there." You are meant to awaken to it. Connect with it. Nurture it as if it were a beloved child of your own. Feed it, coddle it, allow it to speak. Listen to it. Learn from it. Allow its presence to grow and blossom within you.

Your soul is also meant to see others as souls and connect with them as such. Additionally, your soul is meant to reflect and emanate the Love that it is—the Love that you are—the Love of God.

—Dr. Linda Humphreys

PART III

"UNSEEN" FORCES and INFLUENCES

Chapter 14

Energy Centers

If you want to find the secrets of the universe, think in terms of energy, frequency, and vibration.

—*Nikola Tesla*

Another aspect within the realm of the unconscious / subconscious is the *Energy Body*. These subtle energies are what constitute one's aura, prana, and qi (or chi).

Energy Body

Barbara Ann Brennan, author of *Hands of Light*, writes about the seven components of the Energy Body:

- **Etheric:** Extends one-quarter to two inches from the physical body. This is what is captured in Kirlian photography.

- **Emotional:** Extends one to three inches from the physical body.

- **Mental Energy:** Stores our mental processes, judgments, perceptions, and thoughts. This energy extends three to eight inches from the physical body.

- **Astral Body:** Assists in the detection of more subtle energy perceptions. It extends six inches to one foot from one's physical body.

- **Etheric Template Body:** It is said that this is the template from which your body is formed—like a blueprint. The extension is one and a half to two feet from one's body.

- **Celestial Body:** Described as the spiritual emotional plane. When we experience "The Oneness," spiritual bliss, and both inner- and inter-connections (between you and others), we are connected to the celestial body via this "bridge" to the Divine.

- **Ketheric Template Body:** Described as the mental aspect of the spiritual plane. All of the other bodies are contained within this body, with an extension of up to three and a half feet. We experience this template when we experience our "Divine Knowing."

Chakras

Chakras are energy centers. Some people refer to chakras as the "spiritual spine." Here are the basics from Chakras.info:

> Originating from Sanskrit, [chakras] literally means "wheel" by association with its function as a vortex of spinning energy interacting with various physiological and neurological systems in the body. Chakras are energy centers within the human body that help to regulate all its processes, from organ function to the immune system and emotions. We can commonly count 7 chakras positioned throughout your body, from the base of your spine to the crown of your head. Each chakra has its own vibrational frequency, that is depicted through a specific chakra color, and governs specific functions that help make you, well, human.

The seven chakras are:

Chakra Name	Color	Position	Connections[1]
Root	red	base of spine	grounding, survival, safety
Sacral	orange	below navel	creativity, sexuality, relationships, emotions
Solar Plexus	yellow	stomach	personal power, will, confidence
Heart	green	center of chest	love, empathy, compassion
Throat	blue	base of throat	creative self-expression, speaking one's truth
Brow (Third Eye)	indigo	forehead, above & between eyes	insight, wisdom, inner vision, intuition
Crown	violet / white	top of head	higher consciousness, connection with the Divine

Though I have listed seven chakras, I have heard that there is actually a total of twelve known chakras. I believe there may even be more.

Meridians

According to the teachings of traditional Chinese medicine (TCM), meridian systems (channels or pathways of energy, also known as "qi" or "chi") are the pathways along which the body's vital energy flows. They can also be thought of as a collection of acupuncture points.

There are twelve "principal" meridians and eight "extra" meridians. The governing meridian is among the "extra" meridians, and as such it is viewed as among the most important channels. Its importance is derived from the independent nature of its acupuncture points—which are not part of the twelve principal meridians[2].

---

[1] NOTE: This is a compilation of what I have learned and studied throughout the years from various sources and resources. The Connections column is a partial, cursory listing of properties, gifts, and attributes connected with each chakra.

[2] Source: www.shen-nong.com

If you drew a line of the governing meridian, it would run from the center of your upper lip, up the center of the nose, forehead, over the center of the head, down the center spine, and end at the tailbone.

Your Fingertips

The tips of your fingers emit energy, as is evidenced by Kirlian photography. They are a powerful tool and used in a variety of healing modalities. Your fingertips are elements that can facilitate remarkable transformation when placed on energy points and combined with the power of your intentions, humility (stepping aside), higher vibration states of energy (gratitude, openness), and God / Spirit / Highest Power. They are the tools that are utilized within "The GOD Project" to support the release of negative subconscious programming.

***

In the next chapters, I explain how working with energy centers can assist in unlocking the secrets of your inner subconscious universe.

Chapter 15

Exploring "Unseen"
Forces and Influences with Divining

How fathomless the mystery of the Unseen is!
—Guy de Maupassant

Wondering what was within my subconscious (running 95 percent of my own habits and behaviors), within my energy field—and wondering how that applied to my perceived relationship with God—I decided to literally test myself.

"Proof" via a Lie Detector

I set out to explore the best and most efficient way to do this. I often thought, *If I could find some kind of a detector test, that would be the way to do it.* At that time, the only testing I knew of was using an actual "lie detector." Half-jokingly and half-seriously, I looked into the concept and the mechanics of the "lie detector" device.

The Lie Detector (As I Understand It)

In very simple terms, this is what I learned:

- Our bodies and energy fields respond to unseen forces and influences.

- The nervous system is the channel of electrical energy and controls skeletal muscles.

- When something resonates with us (such as a truthful statement, a thought, specific feeling), we have a physiological response to it via the nervous system.

- When there is dissonance with something, we have a physiological response to it as well.

- In addition to changes in breathing patterns and heart rate, a physiological response can be in the form of micro muscle movements.

- A lie detector test is formally called the Galvanic Skin Response Test.

- This testing device can detect physiological responses, including micro muscle movements and the flow of energy.

- These micro muscle movements and the flow of energy are tracked via graphing.

- A baseline of resonance (truth) and the presence of dissonance (falsehood) can be discerned and are the first things discerned.

- Upon questioning, if there is resonance (truth) present, no marked movements of micro muscles are detected. The lines on the graph will be stable. This indicates that there is no disruption or obstruction of the flow of energy. It is equivalent to getting an affirmative response.

- Upon questioning, if there is dissonance (falsehood) present, marked micro muscle movements are detectable. The lines on the graph dip downward and waiver. This indicates that there is a disruption or obstruction in the flow of electrical energy, resulting in blocked energy. It is equivalent to getting a "not affirmative" response.

Not having a Galvanic Skin Response device at my disposal, I searched for other ways to discern resonance and dissonance within myself—especially as it related to what was running my subconscious "show" regarding my perceived relationship with God. My search lead me to find exactly what I was looking for—a modality that is:

- Accurate,
- Practical,

- Portable,

- Something I could quickly and easily master,

- Something I could do myself or could find support for, and

- Not prohibitive financially.

Divining / Applied Kinesiology / Muscle Testing

The best and most accurate way I have found to test one's energy field and unconscious / subconscious programming is commonly called *muscle testing* or *applied kinesiology (AK)*. Regardless of what it is called, I believe it is a form of divining.[3]

While researching the mechanics behind the practice, I learned that the energy that causes weakening of muscles when performing AK / muscle testing / divining is also the same energy that propels the swinging of the pendulum (another modality of resonance and dissonance detection and a form of divining). All of the above modalities operate using the same theory and energy that causes results detected by the Galvanic Skin Response device.

Mechanics of Divining / AK / Muscle Testing (As I Understand It)

In very simple terms, this is what I learned (note that there is overlap with the Lie Detection process):

- Our bodies and energy fields respond to unseen forces and influences.

- The nervous system is the channel of electrical energy and controls skeletal muscles.

- When there is resonance with something (for example, a truthful statement, a thought), we can have a physiological response to it.

---

[3] I find it interesting that certain forms of applied kinesiology (AK) are referred to as "divining" or "divination" (examples include divining rod and dowsing rod). I truly believe the word "divination" does have a root (literally and metaphorically) with the Divine. I view AK as a gift from the Divine with which to access the Divine Knowing Within.

- When there is dissonance with something, we can have a physiological response to it as well.

- In addition to changes in breathing patterns and heart rate, a physiological response can be in the form of micro muscle movements.

- Divining can detect changes in the micro muscle movements and the flow of energy.

- With divining, a baseline of resonance (truth) and the presence of dissonance (falsehood) can be discerned and are the first things discerned.

- Upon questioning, if there is resonance (truth) present, no marked movements of micro muscles are detected; electrical energy flows freely and the muscles will test "strong." This indicates that there is no disruption or obstruction of the flow of energy and no blocked energy. It is equivalent to getting an affirmative response.

- Upon questioning, if there is dissonance (falsehood) present, marked micro muscle movements are detected. This indicates a disruption or obstruction in the flow of electrical energy, resulting in blocked energy, causing the muscles to test "weak." It is equivalent to getting a "not affirmative" response.

You can test your energetic alignment with physical "tangible things" (such as a food or supplement) and "intangible things" (like thoughts, ideas, or emotions). This type of testing helps you decipher whether something is *energetically* congruent / beneficial / in resonance with / or present (as it relates to thoughts, ideas, emotions) for you and your energy system—resulting in a *strong* or *yes* response.

Additionally, you can use this form of testing to help you decipher whether something is *energetically* incongruent / not beneficial / in dissonance with / or not present (as it relates to thoughts, ideas, emotions) for you and your energy system—resulting in a *weak* or *not strong* response.

Divining as a "GOD Project" Tool

I consider the tool of divining to be my personal and portable "lie detector." Like a *lie detector*, it discerns truth / resonance and falsehood / dissonance. Additionally, divining is a tool that can be used to discover and discern energetic blocks and imbalances that are present within your subconscious / unconscious and your energy field.

In the context of the "GOD Project," divining is used to discover what negative and/or challenging beliefs / programs, blocks and imbalances are present that contribute to a perceived "distance" between you and God. Additionally, you can use divining techniques to discover which positive beliefs / programs are missing—and contributing to your perception of not experiencing your desired positive relationship with God.

How to Divine

There are over a dozen ways to conduct divining / AK / muscle testing without having to use a "lie detector" / Galvanic Skin Response apparatus. You can have another person facilitate the divining, or you can divine by yourself. In Chapter 21 you will learn one example each of two methods—one that requires two people and another method that you can do by yourself. Additional methods are explained in *GETTING GOD*™ ~ *The Guidebook—Exploration & Conscious Connection Support for Your "GOD Project"*.

Chapter 16

Energy Tools and Qualities of Transformation

Always bear in mind that your resolution to succeed
is more important than any one thing.
—Abraham Lincoln

"Setting intentions" is something frequently mentioned and practiced in a lot of self-help books, workshops, conferences, metaphysical materials, and the like. When I first began my inward journey, I noticed that I would physically bristle when I heard that phrase.

Wanting to explore why I was reacting in such a way, I did some reflection. I soon realized that the concept of *intentions* had confused me for a very long time. I struggled to understand why people would set intentions, what "setting intentions" actually meant, and how to set intentions in an effective manner. I was also challenged with finding the appropriate vibration / energy that would enhance my intentions.

Setting Intentions

As I shared in Part I of this book, the religious *Baltimore Catechism* textbooks had a strong influence on me and left strong impressions with me. One of the sayings I remember seeing in a religious book was "The road to hell is paved with good intentions." Along with that saying was an illustration of a stairway. On each of the outward-facing sides of the stairs was the word *Intention.* The area at the top of the staircase was labeled *Heaven,* with the obligatory white clouds, angels, and God portrayed as an old man with a white beard, sitting down and watching what was happening below. The bottom of the stairway led to what was labeled *Hell,* with the obligatory flames, red and horned demons with pitchforks, and, of course, Satan.

Fast-forward to the time of great popularity and focus on manifesting things, which came to the forefront with the popularity of the book and the movie *The Secret*. Books and workshops about "manifestation," "laws" of attracting things, affirmations and mantra creations and recitations, and so on were prominent within metaphysical circles. At that time, I still had the energetic vibrations of the imagery I described above running rampant within me. When I was asked to state a simple intention regarding manifesting something, I would frequently say, "There is no way in *hell* I would *ever* set an intention! I could end up in hell—because even good intentions can lead me straight to hell!"

I thought of all of the times I had intentions and said I would do something and, for whatever reason, whatever I was intending to happen did not come about. I realized that I did not follow through, I forgot about my intentions, and so on. Upon deeper reflection, I realized I was using my "intentions" as yet another weapon against myself—especially as it related to *not* "manifesting" something. New Age guilt can be just as inwardly insidious and brutal as Catholic guilt.

I would set the intention to do something—fast, meditate, journal—as a way to get something to physically manifest in my life (increases in my bank accounts, relationships), and I was always using it as a bargaining chip, a quid pro quo, a leverage tool with God/the universe. Energetically, it was as if I were stating to God/the universe, "I'll do _____ if you do/give me _____" or "If you do/give me _____ then I will _____."

I now realize that intentions do carry energy: the energy in which they are created and the energy in which they are held by the person creating the intention. This energy warrants conscious exploration and, in some cases, adjustments.

Energetic adjustment can be made to put something more in alignment, not only with the desired outcome, but in keeping the highest and best benefit for both the intention setter and for those affected by and involved with the intention.

Intentions are meant to be stated in an affirmative way. An example of an *affirmative way* means instead of stating "*not* being as confused" (what you *don't* want and using the word *not*)—state *clarity* (what you *do* want). Another example: Instead of stating "*not* being so disconnected from God"—state *experiencing connection with God.*

Energetic Qualities of Intentions / Energetically Infused Goals

- Direct positive and affirmative focus

- Commitment to being open and vulnerable

- Commitment to transformation

- Willingness / flexibility / adaptability

- Grounding in the "here and now"

- Projection of positive energy and the image of a positive outcome into your future

Examples of Intentions[4]

- It is my intention to release and let go of blocks or barriers, of any kind and on all levels, that I have created which separate me from the experiencing God as love and that God loves me.

- My intention is to experience God's love for me and to love God more fully.

Affirmations

Affirmations are positive statements. The purpose of using affirmations is to anchor the positive energy of your intentions in the "here and now" and to project it into the future. Additionally, by using

---

[4] In *GETTING GOD*™ ~ *The Guidebook—Exploration & Conscious Connection Support for Your "GOD Project"*, I offer detailed guidance for creating the most effective intentions that relate to your "GOD Project." I also provide more examples.

some specific wording, they can support greater energetic alignment with your intentions.

There is a huge energetic difference between wishful thinking and an affirmation. Wishful thinking begins with words such as *I want to, I hope to, It would be nice if*, and so on. The energy with these types of statements is wistful, weak, and filled with doubt. It states a longing for something to happen. It also leaves a lot of space for the energy of something *not* to happen because the implied energy is "It would be nice if _____ happens, *but…*"

Every time the word or energy of the word *but* is used in these types of statements, you create conflicting or competing energies. Conflicting or competing energies negates affirmations. You do not want to leave any invitation for conflicting energy when creating affirmations.

To create energetically strong affirmations, some specific wording can be beneficial. I found the following helpful when creating my affirmations:

- Begin each sentence with "I Am." This is done to call forward the God / Spirit / Highest Power / I AM presence within you and align it with the God / Spirit / Highest Power / I Am presence throughout.

  - Another reason to use *I Am* instead of *I will* or *I am going to*: It supports being in the "here and now" and does not postpone things into a nebulous and / or unspecified future.

- State the action word or verb in the present / present-progressive tense. Another way of stating this is to use verbs that end with *–ing* (enjoy*ing*, play*ing*, danc*ing*). This supports anchoring the energy in the "here and now" and paves the way, energetically, for your future. (See Examples of Affirmations below.)

Another key element of affirmations is to keep them within the realm of possibility for you. Some workshops and training programs

I have attended suggest creating affirmations using this guideline: Make them (at least) 50 percent possible or believable. For example, *I am graduating from medical school with honors* won't work for me because I have no medical aptitude and am squeamish at the sight of blood. That affirmation is *not* within the realm of possibility nor is it something that is believable to me.

Having said that, I do believe in miracles, and I always avail myself to being open and receptive for miracles at all times. I feel it is important for you to do the same.

Energetic Qualities of Affirmations

- Being positive / supportive / uplifting / affirming

- Commitment to transformation

- Openness / willingness / flexibility / adaptability

- Grounding in the "here and now"

- Projection of positive energy and the image of successful outcomes into your future

Examples of Affirmations

- "I Am open and receptive to transforming my relationship with God in an easy and gentle manner."

- "I Am enjoying sharing my love with God and feeling God's love for me."

Your "North Star" Vision Creation Story

I define a *vision creation* as a compilation of affirmations that are compiled in a way that creates a positive energetic response within. I view it as a trade-in and upgrade from one's old victim story. It can be a list of affirmations or a narrative. You can add color, pictures, or anything you can think of that will enhance the positive energy you are consciously creating. (See *Example of a "North Star" Vision Creation Story* on the next page.)

Again, I do believe in miracles, and I want to be open and receptive to them at all times. That is why I like to include a supportive addendum at the end of my vision stories.

In many of the transformational programs, courses, and workshops I have taken since the 1980s, the following success mindset left an impression on me. Though various people state it in different ways, here is the central idea. After stating your affirmations and/or creating your vision story, add something akin to the following statement:

I _____ (embrace/claim/affirm) this, or something even more _____ (grand/magnificent/delightful), for the _____ (greatest/maximum/highest/grandest) _____ (benefit/blessing/outcome) for myself and others.

Energetic Qualities of "North Star" Vision Creation Stories

- Being positive/supportive/uplifting/affirming
- Commitment to transformation
- Openness/willingness/flexibility/adaptability
- Grounding in the "here and now"
- Projection of positive energy and successful outcomes into your future

Example of a "North Star" Vision Creation Story

I Am excited! I Am experiencing an amazingly loving relationship with God. I Am experiencing God's love for me. I Am being supported, guided, and loved. Each and every day, I Am witnessing and experiencing increasing awareness of these Truths ...

I affirm all of this and even more—much greater and grander than what I can possibly imagine—for the maximum benefit to myself, others, and the entire planet.

Prayer = Talking to God

Based on an informal survey I conducted, there are a myriad of reasons for talking, but the top five reasons are:

1. To be heard,

2. To express yourself,

3. To share your perspective of a story,

4. To vent, and

5. To share a grievance.

Talking does not necessarily mean that you engage in a dialogue. Talking can be a one-sided tirade, a monologue, a soliloquy.

Simply stated, I view prayer as talking *to* God / Spirit / Highest Power. Admittedly, on more than a few occasions and while in the guise of praying, I have been guilty of having my own one-sided tirades, monologues, and soliloquies directed toward God.

These forms of communication are not effective in human relationships—especially when they are the main style of "conversation." I realized that they were not effective when talking to God, either. At the end of doing this form of so called "prayer," I was left feeling more frustrated and alone. This contributed to my sense of separation from the Divine.

Upon reflection, I asked myself, *Are my prayers effective? If not, why not? If yes, why?* Wanting to dissect this further, I asked myself, *What is the desired effect of prayer? Is there something that I could do differently that would contribute to a more enhanced experience of praying? If yes, what makes a prayer / praying effective?*

After studying different types of prayer, I decided to experiment and change how I prayed. Below are some of the things I learned and experienced, and what I believe does contribute to a greater sense of openness and connectedness while praying.

Energetic Qualities of Praying

- Honesty
- Openness / vulnerability
- Willingness to transform
- Affirming
- Gratitude
- Trusting God / Spirit / Highest Power
- Flexibility

Elements to Include While Praying

- Address God.

- Speak from your heart.

- Express humility (see Chapter 5); acknowledge God as God / Spirit / Highest Power, and express gratitude for that.

- Acknowledge openness to God's infinite wisdom and divine plan for everyone involved in the situation.

- Listen.

- Express even more gratitude.

- Affirm: Thank you. I am grateful. And so it is. Amen!

- Trust in God that the best thing for all souls involved will transpire.

Example of Effective Prayer

God / Spirit / Highest Power, I Am open and receptive to bringing forth whatever can be released and will make a significant difference with my healing and transformation at this time. I know You are with me and guiding this process in an easy and gentle manner. I pray for deeper understanding, greater awareness, and opening up to Your loving presence in my life. Thank you for Your love and support, now and always. I affirm this and even more delightful and joyful awarenesses and experiences, for my greatest benefit and for the greatest benefit of all others as well. Thank you. I Am grateful.

And so it is. Amen.

Meditation = Listening to God

Simply stated, meditation means *listening* to God/Spirit/Highest Power. It does not mean listening for what you hope to hear. Meditation is not about manipulating anything to get a specifically desired outcome. It is not meant to uphold or support your thinking mind's thoughts, stories, perceived "wrongs," and other misperceptions.

Meditation is about being open and vulnerable enough to accept whatever comes forward without interference from the thinking mind. It is also about a willingness to listen for and to hear Truth (capital "T") rather than what the thinking mind/ego/human personality wants to label as truth and wants to hear. It is a time to turn within and tune into your Intuition, which I believe is The Voice of God. It is meant to liberate you from the thinking mind and support you in connecting with The Mind of God Within.

While meditation is often described in various ways, including a "mindfulness" practice, for those new to the concept and practice, you can view it in these ways:

- Meditation is a mind-*less*-ness practice—an opportunity to practice disconnecting from the head chattering/monkey mind/munching mind—creating stillness within to be open to not only perceiving God's Inner Guidance but also being able to clearly attune to it.

- Mediation is a mind-*full*-ness practice—After being able to quiet the chattering mind, it creates space in which you can connect with The Oneness—and *fill* your mind with The Mind of God.

Either way, meditation is a practice—and requires practice. When I make it a habit to meditate—even for a few minutes on a regular basis, I find that my body and my psyche actually begin to crave doing it. I feel a bit "off" if I do not take a few minutes to simply attune inwardly and be still. The more I meditate, the more I want to meditate.

How to Begin to Meditate
Quiet your mind. Tune in to the rhythm of your heartbeat, or to the rise and fall of your chest, while you deeply inhale and exhale.

If your attention wanders and you begin to engage with your thinking mind, be gentle with yourself and simply return to the stillness within.

Optional: At the beginning of the meditation, you can state your intention to receive inner knowing about a specific topic. You can also ask a question, request guidance, information, support, and / or inspiration.

Energetic Qualities of Meditation
- Openness / vulnerability
- Acceptance
- Willingness
- Humility (see Chapter 5)

Examples of Meditation Queries (Optional)
- What does God / Spirit / Highest Power want to reveal to me about _____?
- What is God's True Nature?
- How can I become more _____?

Moving Forward
Change can be quite threatening to some people. Any change.

After releasing old and ineffective energy blocks and imbalances (both conscious and unconscious / subconscious) and incorporating new insights and ways of being within yourself (toward God, others, and to life and living in general), moving forward is the next step.

Moving forward takes courage. That is especially true when unhappy, angry, fearful, and judgmental people notice a shift in you. Some may feel threatened because your reaction to the inter-action between the two of you is no longer the same or predictable. Your responses and interactions become unpredictable—and this can be quite unsettling for them. Some may want to remind you of your past in an attempt to keep you bound, captive, held hostage, and forever tethered to your past. They want to define you based on their perceptions / misperceptions of their—and your—past. They view you through their rearview mirror.

Actually, all this does is keep *them* tethered to *their* own past—*their* own misperceptions and distortions based on *their* own inner negativity. They are trying to hoist their negative perceptions of their past into their—and your—present and future. These people want to hold on to their own past and use it as a weapon to keep you in place. That "place" happens to be within their own negativity, judgments, unhappiness, and fear. They think they can use that "place" as leverage to control you. In fact, it only serves as a means of constriction and confinement within them. It holds *them* hostage and bound to *their* past.

Others, who have not yet moved forward themselves, may say things such as:

- "How dare you rock the boat!"
- "I remember when you said (or did)_____."
- "You acted like _____."
- "I remember the time when you were _____."
- "I will never forget the time when you said (or did) _____."

- "I will never forgive you for _____."
- "I will never forget or forgive you for the time when you _____."

Energetic Qualities of Moving Forward

- Having determination / resolve
- Embracing fortitude / perseverance
- Loving and caring for everyone involved, including yourself
- Releasing
- Allowing
- Being nonjudgmental

Examples of Moving Forward

When confronted and challenged by those in fear, resistance, and judgment who are experiencing anger, unhappiness, and discontent within their own lives, it would behoove you to focus your energy and attention on your continuing transformation. Focus on your intentions and commitment to your growth and upliftment. In other words, "Keep on keeping on."

A more positive reframing or perceiving of others' reactive and negative responses to your evolution can be applied to the degree of others' reactions (such as anger, disturbance, reactiveness, defensiveness, and attacking). Neutrally observing the amount and / or intensity of others' negative reactions can be a great tool for you to measure how much you have grown, been uplifted, and transformed. More simply stated, the strength of others' negative reactions can reflect, proportionally, the degree to which you have transformed.

Some things to consider: Sometimes "allowing" and "releasing" may mean allowing other people to be themselves and releasing any and all judgments you may have against *them* for how they are reacting to your transformation. At times, it may mean releasing the relationship—allowing your continuing upliftment and trans-formation with freedom from their negative reactions, energy, repercussions, and interference.

At all times, try your utmost to be loving and caring toward everyone—especially those who are on a different path in life. May **everything** serve as a blessing and lesson for you. Remember, at all times, try your utmost to be grateful for the gifts and blessings that negatively reactive people have been in your life, and bless them and their journeys. Move forward on your own path—loving them and yourself—along the way.

—Dr. Linda Humphreys

PART IV

The GOD PROJECT

Chapter 17

Elements of "The GOD Project"

It takes a deep commitment to change and an even deeper commitment to grow.

—Ralph Ellison

To keep things simple, I have distilled the "The GOD Project" process into several key theoretical and practical elements. Each of these elements is listed as a step, and the process of each step is covered in more detail in individual chapters.

"GOD Project" Overview

When you think about God and how you perceive your relationship with God, you will want to:

Step 1: Evaluate and Determine

In this first step, you will consider:

- How you feel / what you perceive now,
- Your perceived stress or challenge level,
- What you want to experience,
- Your intentions for this relationship,
- Affirmations in support of your intentions, and
- Creating a vision of what you want to experience.

Step 2: Explore

Next, you will explore your:

- Religious / church-based indoctrinations,
- Family of origin indoctrinations,

- Perceptions of parental figures' relationship with God,

- Who your most challenging parental figure is/was, and what you perceived are/were that person's challenging characteristics, and

- Your perception of your God figure's challenging characteristics.

Step 3: Examine Your Thoughts and Feelings

Then you will examine your:

- Judgments and resentments,

- Your shadow self (what you do not want to own about yourself),

- Positive thoughts, feelings, and energy, and

- Negative thoughts, feelings, and energy.

Step 4: Expose Via Divining

Now you will uncover your subconscious thoughts by:

- Using the beginning session protocol for *all* sessions,

- Divining which statement to clear first … next … next, and

- Divining for more information.

Step 5: Eliminate Through Energetic Clearing and Releasing

Next you will clear and release by:

- Divining which energetic clearing modality to use,

- Using the energetic clearing modality indicated,

- Addressing "negative/challenged" subconscious and conscious thoughts and energy,

- Addressing energetic blocks and imbalances causing separation from "positive" ("lack of positive") subconscious and conscious thoughts and energy.

Step 6: Empower

Finally, you will empower yourself by:

- Using supportive "GOD Project" relationship practices,

- Continuing to study, investigate, meditate about, ask for guidance and clarity about, and seek the True Nature of God,

- "Checking in" within, connecting with yourself, connecting with Spirit, and connecting with Spirit and you as a whole, and

- Getting additional support on all levels.

Additionally, it is my prayer that you *emerge* with these ongoing intentions for:

- New energy,

- Greater clarity,

- Less levels of stress / challenge as it relates to your perceived relationship with God,

- Improved perception and experience of the True Nature of God,

- More positive experiences of love toward God, yourself, and within yourself,

- More positive experiences of love toward others, and

- Greater openness to all of the good, the blessings, the riches, the beauty, and all the love and magic that God / the universe has in store for you.

More detailed suggestions, examples, and additional support materials can be found in *GETTING GOD™ ~ The Guidebook— Exploration & Conscious Connection Support for Your "GOD Project"*.

Chapter 18

Step 1: Evaluate and Determine

Knowing yourself is the beginning of all wisdom.
—Aristotle

As with any project and experiment, it is always good to establish a baseline in which you can measure your progress. "The GOD Project" is no different. As part of your "GOD Project," journal your responses to the queries below.

Evaluate

Start by using the following as the baseline question:

When you think about God and how you perceive your relationship with God …

- *How do you feel?*

- *What do you perceive now?*

- *What is your perceived stress or challenge level now?*

Stress / Challenge Evaluation

Find a quiet time and space. Take a moment to connect to your body through deep breathing. Connect with your feelings. Silently read the questions below. Journal your responses.

- On a scale of 1–10 (1 = ever so slightly stressed / challenged; 10 = deeply, disturbingly stressed / challenged), rate the following:

  - *How much of a challenge is / how much stress are you currently experiencing with your perceived relationship with God?*

○ When you think about the current status of your relationship with God, what amount of stress do you experience within?

○ How blocked / closed off do you feel regarding receiving love from God?

○ How blocked / closed off do you feel regarding sending love to God?

○ How much frustration do you feel regarding your relationship with God?

Add other statements or observations about your stresses and challenges.

Determine

With any project or experiment, it is always a good idea to establish what direction you want to be going in—what you are working toward.

Find a quiet time and space. Take a moment to connect to your body through deep breathing. Connect with your feelings. Silently read the question below. Journal your responses.

What do you want to experience in your relationship with God?

Mindset of Success

Again, in many of the transformational programs, courses, and workshops I have taken since the 1980s, the following success mindset left an impression on me and I like to incorporate it whenever possible. Though various people state it in different ways, here is the central idea:

If this _____ (book, program, project) were to be _____ (immensely, wildly, greatly) successful, what would you experience?

Now, it is your turn. Answer the following:

If this _____ *(book, program, project)*
were to be _____ *(immensely, wildly, greatly)*
successful, I would experience _____.

You can use these techniques to explore other parts of your "God Project"[5]:

- **Your Intentions.** Using your responses to the last statement above can assist you in creating your intentions. Create your "GOD Project" intentions now.

- **Your Affirmations.** Using your intentions above can assist you in creating affirmations. Create your "GOD Project" affirmations now.

- **Your "North Star" Vision Creation Story.** Using your affirmations can assist you in your Vision Creation. Create your "GOD Project" vision now.

---

[5] See Chapter 16, "Energy Tools and Qualities of Transformation" and the ***GETTING GOD*™ ~ *The Guidebook—Exploration & Conscious Connection Support for Your "GOD Project"*** for additional information and support.

Chapter 19

Step 2: Explore

When I discover who I am, I'll be free.
—Ralph Ellison

I believe it is imperative to consciously explore your memory to trace the root cause of your sense and perception of "separation" from God / Spirit / Highest Power. As part of your "God Project," you will be asked to explore what you learned about God, how you learned it, and who you learned it from. You will also be asked to journal your responses to the reflections and queries that follow.

Indoctrinations

Looking into the religion in which you were born and the belief systems (dogmas / indoctrinations / programs) that were instilled in you as you were growing up is the best place to start when exploring your sense of separation.

Religion / Church Indoctrination. In the books, songs, and movies you were exposed to in your religion, church, affiliated events and gatherings, catechism, and Saturday or Sunday school, how was God described? How are you, in relationship to God, described?

Family of Origin Indoctrination. If your mother was present during your upbringing, how did she describe God? (If your mother was not present, how did the most influential female figure during your upbringing, describe God?)

If your father was present during your upbringing, how did he describe God? (If your father was not present, how did the most influential male figure during your upbringing, describe God?)

Perceptions of Relationships with God

The ways your parental influences related to God—and your perceptions of their relationships with God—affected your perception of your own relationship with God.

Perceptions of Parental Figures' Relationships with God. If you were to describe the relationship your mother or the most influential female in your life had with God—based purely on your perspective and perceptions—how would you describe it?

If you were to describe the relationship your father or the most influential male in your life had with God—based purely on your perspective and perceptions—how would you describe it?

Perceptions of Your Relationship with God. If you were to describe your relationship with God while you were growing up—based purely on your perspective and perceptions—how would you describe it?

Today, if you were to describe your relationship with God—based purely on your perspective and perceptions—how would you describe it?

Looking back, did your relationship with God reflect your relationship with your most challenging parental figure?

Challenging Characteristics and Relationships

Challenging relationship characteristics can be serially repeated and experienced. Explore the challenging common denominator(s) within your relationships.

Challenging Parental Figure. Which relationship did you find to be more challenging while you were growing up: the relationship with your mother (or an influential female figure) or with your father (or an influential male figure)? How would you describe the characteristics of the person you were more challenged by?

Challenging God Figure Characteristics. Does your most challenging parental figure or influential person possess the same characteristics that you attribute to God? Based on your experiences, opinions, and perceptions, what do your most challenging parental figure and God have in common?

Challenging Relationships. Reflecting on your most challenging relationships, what did / do they have in common with your most challenging parental figure or influential person? With God?

I believe there is a correlation between our negative perceptions / misperceptions of our most influential parental figures, of God, and ourselves. The order in which these appeared in your conscious and / or subconscious does not actually matter. Regardless of the order, they produce a "looping" effect: As one aspect is affected, so are the others.

BOTTOM LINE: For a clearer, healthier, more accurate, and more "positive" perception of your relationship with God to manifest, whatever is muddled, unhealthy, inaccurate, imbalanced, challenging, and "negative" must be identified and removed.

Chapter 20

Step 3: Examine Your Thoughts and Feelings

The unexamined life is not worth living.

—Socrates

Although you are not your "story," within your story resides aspects of you that need to be addressed and energetically released and cleared so you can transform and spiritually evolve. In this step, you will examine thoughts and feelings that contributed to the creation and perpetuation of your story of you and of your relationship with God.

Using paper separate from your journal (because these pages will be shredded after your clearings), write what comes forward for you as you read through the following ideas. Go within, and be as honest as possible.

Judgments and Resentments

Consider the following: *What judgments and resentments do you hold against your most challenging parent/influential person? Against God? Against yourself?*

Relationship "Mirrors" and Projections

I have observed that relationships can act as mirrors of both conscious and subconscious feelings as well as attitudes, beliefs, perceptions, and misperceptions. Quite often, what we do not want to accept in ourselves we project (or place) onto others—especially if we deem the things we do not want to accept as "negative."

This is not a new concept. It is a basic principle of psychology. (I learned this in Psychology 101.) I have, however, experienced and witnessed it firsthand—specifically and directly as it relates to perceptions and misperceptions of God.

What Do You Not Want to Own About Yourself?

Holding the mirror up to yourself can assist in acknowledging and owning your shadow side. It is a vital step in your transformational process. This step requires rigorous honesty. By bringing light to your shadow side, it helps clear negative energy and paves the way for you to, subsequently, acknowledge and own your own Inner Divinity. Continue to journal your responses to the following questions on separate paper.

- *What do you perceive are aspects of your "shadow" side—the part of your personality you judge as "bad," "wrong," and/or "unacceptable"?*

- *What are you hoping is not true of your personality (yet most likely is)?*

- *What personality characteristics are you most ashamed of?*

- *If someone were to describe your personality, what terms would trigger a defensive response within you?*

Plus …

- *What do you perceive are aspects of your "positive" side, the part of your personality you judge as "not me"—"I am too much of a sinner to be considered _____"—and/or "unacceptable"?*

- *What are you hoping is true of your personality?*

- *What personality characteristics are you most proud of, but fear they are not actually true?*

- *If someone were to describe your personality, what "positive" terms would trigger a defensive response within you?*

Positive and Negative Aspects

I believe a holistic approach to removing blocks and imbalances in the conscious and subconscious mind involves addressing the presence of "Negative / Challenged" statement energetics, programs, and vibrations, *plus* the "Lack of Positive" statement energetics, programs, and vibrations. I assert that both—the presence of a "negative" *plus* the absence of a "positive"—are equally detrimental, and equal attention must be placed on the exploration, release, and clearing of *both* the presence of negative energy and the absence of positive energy.

Exploration Statements

In this book and the accompanying *Guidebook*, I provide statements you can use as a springboard and catalyst for the creation of your own statements. As statements occur to you, write them down.

The lists I have provided are not all-inclusive and are not in any specific order or hierarchy. They are merely samplings. Sources of additional statements include:

- What you journaled about during the "Explore" and "Examine" segments of the process (see Chapters 19 and 20)

- What you want to be "True"

- What you fear is true

- What you fear is not true

- Whatever thought about God stirs emotion within you (both positive and negative)

The number of statements and the exact statements that need to be cleared vary for each individual. As more layers are revealed and cleared, even more statements and corresponding energetic vibrations may be revealed. As I stated earlier, our perceived challenges can have multiple layers—like an onion—that need to be peeled away one layer at a time. This is also akin to removing the prickly leaves of an artichoke to reveal the soft heart within. To get the most transformative value out of this process, it is best to be as vulnerable, open, and honest with yourself as possible. There is no judgment—so go for the greatest amount and level of clearing, releasing, and transformation possible for you at this time.

Remember...

This is not a mental/thinking discernment process. This is not a processing of any "story." This is not a "processing" process. It is a process of trusting what is energetically identified by using energy-identifying tools. If you want to use a mind, allow your God Mind—your Divine Mind—to lead this process.

Sample Statements

We impose and infuse energy and vibrations onto words. In this transformational context, and as in all areas of life, words do matter.

While some of the statements and concepts listed in the sample statements may seem redundant, there are reasons why certain concepts are separated and distinguished. To illustrate this, consider the following statements: "God loves me unconditionally," "God accepts me unconditionally," and "God loves and accepts me exactly as I am."

Though your thinking mind may rationalize that love and acceptance equal unconditional love, the thinking mind tends to compartmentalize things. Your thinking mind can identify love and acceptance as two separate things and distinct things and rationalize reasons for doing so. This compartmentalization leads to the creation of two (or more) separate and distinct layers. It important to realize that each word carries specific vibrations.

Additionally, in combination statements such as "God loves and accepts me exactly as I am," the combination of the words and vibrations of "love" plus "accepts" plus "exactly as I am" carries a different and distinct vibration separate and apart from segregated individual statement components.

When you create your statements, do not censor yourself. Write whatever comes forward and into your awareness. If you have an exact replication of a specific statement, you can delete the exact repetitive statement. Having said that, if you find yourself consistently repeating a specific statement, it is most likely an indication that the specific statement and its vibration is what wants and needs to be addressed—perhaps even first. You can verify all of this through divining (see Chapter 21).

Divining Statements

In the following charts, I have provided some sample "Lack of Positive Statements" and "Negative / Challenged Statements." In addition to what you create for yourself, you will find many more statements, assistive formatting, and some additional information in *GETTING GOD™ ~ The Guidebook—Exploration & Conscious Connection Support for Your "GOD Project."*

Statement Lists Format

The format of the statements lists was designed to support easy tracking of the statements. There is no particular statement hierarchy, order, or grouping. Each chart page has the following:

- Type of Statement (Lack of Positive or Negative / Challenged)

- Page number

- Fifteen statements broken down into three groups (A, B, C) of five statements (1-5) for easy tracking

- A place to note when you were "Challenged" as indicated via divining

  - If test *weak* or *no* regarding a positive statement on a "Lack of Positive Statements" chart

  - If you test *strong* or *yes* regarding a negative statement on a "Negative / Challenged Statements" chart

○ If you test *strong* or *yes* for needing to know more information about the energetic

• A place to notate the energetic was cleared and released

What You Will Be Tracking

During your GOD Project, you will be tracking which energetic statement best represents your "Challenged" energetic blocks and imbalances—and those that are not a challenge *plus* statement energetics what indicate you need to know more information. You will also be tracking the energetic clearing and release.

Challenged Energetics

"Lack of Positive Statements"

• While divining, if you get a *strong* or *yes* response, you can leave the "Challenged" box clear or mark the box with a "0." (I left the box blank because it was easier for me to clearly spot the boxes that were checked.) These statements contain the subconscious/unconscious and conscious thoughts, energy, and vibration that resonate as what you hold as *True*.

• If you get a *weak* or *no* response, mark the *Challenged* box with a "check." These statements represent energetic dissonance and what you hold within your subconscious/unconscious and conscious thoughts, energy, and vibration as *False* or *Not True*.

"Negative/Challenged Statements"

• While divining, if you get a *weak* or *no* response, mark the box with a "0." These statements contain the subconscious/unconscious and conscious thoughts, energy, and vibration that resonate as what you hold as *False or Not True*.

• If you get a *strong* or *yes* response, mark the *Challenged* box with a "check." These statements contain the subconscious

/ unconscious and conscious thoughts, energy, and vibration that resonate as what you hold as *True*.

Need to Know More Information (Any Statement)

- While divining, if you get a *strong* or *yes* response after inquiring if you need to know more information, within the *Challenged* box either add an "I," circle the "check," or create your own notation.

Clearing and Releasing

In Chapter 22, you will learn how to clear and release energetic blocks and imbalances.

"Lack of Positive Statements"

- When a "Lack of Positive Statement" energetic clearing and release has taken place, it means that the energetic block and/or imbalance towards resonance with the positive statement and associated energy has been removed.

"Negative / Challenged Statements"

- When a "Negative / Challenged Statements" energetic clearing and release has taken place, it means that whatever negative energetic block and/or imbalance which created resonance with the negative / challenged statement within your subconscious / unconscious and/or energy field has been cleared.

Within the *Cleared* box, you can either write the date it was cleared, check the box indicating a clearing, or write a "C."

NOTE: Though the statements within the "Lack of Positive Statements" chart are *positive* statements, the intention is to test and track which positive statement energetic is *lacking* or *absent* from one's energy field and / or subconscious.

Lack of Positive Statements (Page 1)	Challenged	Cleared
GROUP A		
1. God loves me.		
2. God and I are One.		
3. God loves me unconditionally.		
4. God loves me no matter what I say, do, think, or how I behave.		
5. God is loving and kind.		
GROUP B		
1. My soul is clean and pure.		
2. God is pleased with me.		
3. God always takes care of me.		
4. God has my back.		
5. God is always with me.		
GROUP C		
1. God is always there for me.		
2. God accepts me unconditionally.		
3. God loves me unconditionally.		
4. God loves and accepts me exactly as I am.		
5. God approves of me.		

Negative/Challenged Statements (Page 1)	Challenged	Cleared
GROUP A		
1. God is angry with me.		
2. God wants to punish me.		
3. God scares me.		
4. God is mean.		
5. God is going to send me to hell.		
GROUP B		
1. I am a poor sinner, and God hates sinners.		
2. God hates me.		
3. God is illusive.		
4. God wants me to suffer.		
5. God is vindictive and spiteful.		
GROUP C		
1. God does not love me.		
2. God's acceptance of me is conditional.		
3. God's love is conditional.		
4. God is always testing me.		
5. I am always failing God's tests.		

Chapter 21

Step 4: Expose Via Divining

Until you make the unconscious conscious,
it will direct your life and you will call it fate.
—Carl Jung

Divining your way into your subconscious/unconscious is intended to be a process that is gentle, supportive, and guided by God/Spirit/Highest Power. It is a way to connect the aspect of God Within to that of God Throughout. There are "check-ins" after each and every step along the way—to make sure you can proceed without any major disturbing upheaval—on any and all levels. It is important to follow the detailed protocols to make sure this is not, in any way, a disruptive process.

Again, like a *lie detector*, divining assists in discovering and discerning truth/resonance and falsehood/dissonance. Divining is also a tool that can be used to discover and discern energetic blocks and imbalances that are present within your subconscious/unconscious and your energy field.

A Friendly Suggestion

Though not a requirement, meditation is an essential tool to utilize and incorporate into one's spiritual tool kit. I have found that meditating—either before or after a clearing and release session—has been extremely beneficial for me.

Two Ways to Divine

There are numerous methods for divining, and you will find many explained in *GETTING GOD*™ ~ *The Guidebook—Exploration & Conscious Connection Support for Your "GOD Project"*.

Here, though, I will share one that requires two people and another method that you can do by yourself. Each method includes some adaptations and options.

Before beginning any step,

1. Stop if you meet resistance,

2. Continue when ready, and

3. *Always* stop if you meet any resistance at any stage.

Two-Person Divining: Outstretched Arm Test (Standing or Sitting)

Begin by having the test taker (testee) outstretch either arm to the side of his or her body.

Tester:

- Set your intention to clearly and easily establish the testee's *strong* (or *yes*) and *weak* (or *no*) baselines. (See below.)

- If testee is standing, stand in front of the testee's raised arm; if testee is seated, sit in chair in front of the testee's raised arm.
  - You can also stand behind the testee.
  - Whichever you choose, continue testing consistently, using the same procedures throughout.

- Place one hand on the shoulder of the side of the testee's outstretched arm; the other hand should be on the testee's outstretched forearm.

- While divining, do not exert brute force. Lightly apply pressure on the testee's forearm. (This is not a test of anyone's physical force, will power, and / or resistance strength.)

Testee:

- Set your intention to clearly and easily establish your *strong* (or *yes*) and *weak* (or *no*) baselines.

- Do not exert tense resistance. Use mild resistance. (Again, this is not a test of anyone's will power, physical strength, and / or resistance strength.)

How to Establish Your Baselines

As previously stated, establishing baselines is an essential process for each and every divining session—and also the first things that must be discerned. With each method, how a *strong / yes* and *weak / no* will feel and look like will be provided.

A. Establish a Clear Strong or Yes Baseline (Two-Person: Outstretched Arm)

Goal / Intention: To get a clear *strong / yes* without muscle strain, force, and so on. While divining, the arm's position should remain *strong* after stating something that is *true*.

- **Testee:** With an outstretched arm, say something that is true while maintaining mild resistance. For example:

    My name is _____.

- **Tester:** Lightly apply pressure on the testee's outstretched forearm.

- **Testee:** Continue to maintain mild resistance.

Baseline Response: Strong or Yes (Two-Person: Outstretched Arm)

- Via divining, if:
    - while testee states something *truthful,* and
    - *simultaneously uses mild resistance*
    - while the tester uses gentle pressure on testee's forearm—
    - and the testee's arm position remains *strong* and does not release—
    - this would indicate a *yes = truthful / congruent* statement.

The tester and testee can now discern what the testee's *yes/affirmative/congruent* divining baseline response looks like and feels like.

Continuation Procedures

- Tester and Testee: Divine if you can proceed.
    - If testee's arm position remains *strong* (*yes*), continue.
    - If testee's arm position becomes *weak* (*no*), refer to **What to Do If You Get a No (Weak) to Proceed** on pages 139–140.

NOTE: If testee's arm position becomes weak (or no) when testing a true statement—stop! Refer to **What to Do If You Are Not Able to Discern Your Yes and No** on page 139.

B. Establish a Clear Weak or No Baseline (Two-Person: Outstretched Arm)

Goal/Intention: To get a clear *weak* or *no* without muscle strain, force, and so on. While divining, the arm's hold should become *weak* and essentially collapse its position after stating something *false*.

- **Testee:** With an outstretched arm, say something that is not true while maintaining mild resistance. For example:

    My name is _____. (State a false name.)

- **Tester:** Lightly apply pressure on the testee's outstretched forearm.

- **Testee:** Continue to maintain mild resistance.

Baseline Response: Weak or No (Two-Person: Outstretched Arm)

- If the testee's arm position becomes *weak* and does not remain strong—this would indicate a *no = not truthful/incongruent* statement.

The tester and testee have now established what the testee's *no/not affirmative/incongruent* divining baseline looks like and feels like.

Continuation Procedures

- Tester and Testee: Divine if you can proceed.

  ○ If testee's arm position remains *strong* (*yes*), continue.

  ○ If testee's arm position becomes *weak* (*no*), refer to **What to Do If You Get a No (Weak) to Proceed** on pages 139–140.

NOTE: If tester and testee are not able to discern between the testee's *yes* and *no*—stop! Refer to **What to Do If You Are Not Able to Discern Your Yes and No** on page139.

Divining by Yourself: Interlocking Fingers

Begin by interlocking your pinkie fingers together. Actually, you can do this with any of your fingers—except for the thumbs. Additionally, you can form interlocking rings with your fingers by interlocking either middle finger and thumbs or index fingers and thumbs.

A. Establish a Clear Strong or Yes Baseline (Interlocking Fingers)

Goal/Intention: To get a clear *strong* or *yes* without muscle strain, force, and so on. The fingers should maintain their locked hold with mild resistance.

- Set your intention to clearly and easily establish your *strong/yes/congruent* baseline.

- With fingers interlocked, maintain mild resistance while saying something that is true—while gently trying to break the hold of the interlocked fingers. For example:

  My name is _____.

- Apply gentle pressure to interlocked fingers while maintaining mild resistance.

- Via divining, if—while stating something *truthful*—your interlocking fingers' hold/link remains *strong* and does not "break"/release with mild resistance and gentle pressure, this would indicate a *yes = truthful/congruent* statement.

   ○ You can now discern what your *yes/affirmative/congruent* divining response baseline response looks like and feels like.

- Divine if you can proceed.

- If you test *strong* or *yes*, continue.

   ○ If you test *weak* or *no*, refer to **What to Do If You Get a No (Weak) to Proceed** on pages 139–140.

- If you get a weak or *no* response when testing the truthful statement—stop!

   ○ Refer to **What to Do If You Are Not Able to Discern Your Yes and No** on page 139.

B. Establish a Clear Weak or No Baseline (Interlocking Fingers)

Goal/Intention: To get a clear *weak* or *no* without muscle strain, force, and so on. The fingers should "break" their locked hold with gentle pressure and mild resistance.

- With fingers interlocked, maintain mild resistance while saying something that is not true—while gently trying to break the hold of the interlocked fingers. For example:

   My name is _____. (State a false name.)

- Via divining, if—while stating something *not truthful*—your interlocking fingers' hold/link becomes *weak* and "breaks"/releases with mild resistance and gentle pressure, this would indicate a *no = not truthful/incongruent* statement.

- You have now established what your *no / not affirmative / incongruent* divining baseline looks like and feels like.

- Via divining, you can now discern between *yes / truthful / congruent* and *no / not truthful / incongruent* responses.

• Next, divine whether or not you can continue at this time.

- If you test *strong* or *yes*, continue.

- If you test *weak* or *no*, refer to **What to Do If You Get a No (Weak) to Proceed** on pages 139–140.

• If you are not able to discern between your *yes* and *no*—stop!

- Refer to **What to Do If You Are Not Able to Discern Your Yes and No** on page 139.

After a clear baseline has been established, you can begin testing anything (food, supplement, statement, idea) to see if it is **energetically** congruent / beneficial / present (as it relates to statements) for you and your energy system and presents a *strong* or *yes* response. Additionally, you can decipher whether something is **energetically** incongruent / not beneficial / not present (as it relates to statements) for you and your energy system, resulting in a *weak* or *no* response.

Summary of Divining Steps with Protocols

Below you will find all of the recommended steps and protocols that will assist you with the divining process during your "GOD Project."

Beginning Session Protocol for All Divining Sessions

For this to be a process of ease and gentleness, it is imperative to establish and adhere to certain protocols.

• Invoke God / Spirit / Highest Power and say a heartfelt prayer.

• State your energetic clearing and releasing intention (verbally or silently).

- For example: It is my intention to partner with God / Spirit / Highest Power and to clearly discern which statement needs/wants to be cleared and released at this time.

- Discern which divining/AK/muscle testing[6] to use by using your intuition.

- Establish your baselines.

Establish Your Baselines (All Divining Sessions)

- State your intention to discern, with ease and clarity, your divining baselines.

- Establish your *strong/yes/congruent* baseline.
  - State something that is *true/factual*. Divine.
  - If you test *strong* or *yes*,
    - You have established what your *yes/true/congruent* statement looks like and feels like while divining.

- If you get a *no* when testing the *true/factual* statement—stop!
  - Refer to **What to Do If You Are Not Able to Discern Your Yes and No** (see below).

- Establish your *weak/no/incongruent* baseline.
  - State something that is *not true*. Divine.
  - If you test *weak* or *no* regarding this *not truthful* statement,
    - you have established your *no/false/incongruent* baseline and
    - you can now discern how your *yes* and *no* feels like and looks like when divining.

- If you are not able to discern between your *yes* and *no*—stop!
  - Refer to **What to Do If You Are Not Able to Discern Your Yes and No** (see next page).

---

[6] From now on, I will only use the word *divine* or *divining*.

What to Do If You Are Not Able to Discern Your *Yes* and *No*

- Drink water. Wait a few minutes and try again.

- Set your intention to experience clarity with discerning *yes* and *no* while divining, in service to your growth, healing, and upliftment.

- This time, think or say out loud: "Yes! Yes! Yes! Yes!" Test for a *yes* baseline. Confirm by stating a true statement. You should experience the same baseline results.

- Now think or say out loud: "No! No! No! No!" Test for a *no* baseline. Confirm by stating a false statement. You should experience the same baseline results.

- Practice, and be patient with yourself.

Divining Continuation Protocol

- Divine if you can proceed.
  - If you test *strong* or *yes*, continue.
  - Ask if you are able to release something at this time. Divine.
    - If you get a *yes* (*strong*), proceed.
    - If you get a *no* (*weak*)—stop![7]
  - Refer to **What to Do If You Get a No (Weak) to Proceed** (see below).

What to Do If You Get a No (Weak) to Proceed

- Drink a glass of water.

- After waiting a few minutes, try again.
  - If you still get a *no* (*weak*), try again another day.
  - Do not continue until you get a *yes* (*strong*) response.

---

[7] From now on, if after getting repeated *no* (weak) responses to: your correct name when attempting to establish your baseline, whether to proceed, or that a clearing took place—stop. Follow the steps in **What to Do If You Get a No (Weak) to Proceed**

- Additionally, consider:
  - going within,
  - praying for clarity and for assistance from God / Spirit / Highest Power,
  - restating your healing intention,
  - being patient and gentle with yourself, and
  - persisting … another day.

Divining Which Statement to Clear First … Next … Next …

Using divining, discern which statement to energetically address, clear, and release first, next, and so on.

Divining Statements Protocol

- Follow the *Beginning Session Protocol for All Divining Sessions.*

- Referring to the statement charts in Chapter 20, ask God / Spirit / Highest Power which type of statement to clear first and discern via divining:
  - "Lack of Positive Statements": Y / N?
  - "Negative / Challenged Statements": Y / N?

- Within the category indicated, ask God / Spirit / Highest Power which of the following to clear first and discern via divining:
  - Group: A (Y / N?), B (Y / N?), C (Y / N?)
  - Number: 1? (Y / N?), 2? (Y / N?), 3? (Y / N?), 4? (Y / N?), 5? (Y / N?)

- Check the "Challenged" box corresponding to the statement indicated.

- Divine to see if more information is needed (see *Divining for More Information* and *Divining for More Information Protocol* on page 142).

○ Reminder: If you are prompted to divine for more information and if there is an indication that the energetic statement was inherited, you can choose to do one of the following within the statement's *Challenged* box:

- Circle the check.
- Place an asterisk or the initial "I" next to the check.
- Create a way to designate the statement as inherited within the *Challenged* box.

• If, after divining, you are given a go-ahead to proceed, begin Step 5 (next chapter).

NOTE: Within one divining statements session, you may move back and forth between both "Negative/Challenged" and "Lack of Positive" statements.

Be patient with yourself and your process.

See *GETTING GOD™ ~ The Guidebook—Exploration & Conscious Connection Support for Your "GOD Project"* for specific examples and session suggestions.

Divining for More Information

Sometimes during my own "GOD Project," I intuitively sensed I needed to know more about the origin of or experience that caused the block and/or imbalance.

Too Much Information or Need to Know?

There were other times that, although I may have been curious about the details that surrounded a block and/or imbalance, no additional information was indicated or required for me (and subsequently for my clients) to know in order for the clearing and releasing to take place.

I believe this is the reason: Some people may be quite "head-y." (At times, I tend to be very immersed within my own head.) Some may still want to be attached to their victim story. Their thinking/ego mind wants "a bone to chew on"; this "munching mind" wants something to gnaw on. Many times, when I ask God/Spirit/Highest

Power if I (or my clients) need to know any additional or detailed information, I receive a *no* when divining.

I view receiving a *no* as a directive from God / Spirit / Highest Power to allow for an easy and gentle rebalancing. I believe that if someone is predisposed to negative perseverations and ruminations of the explicit details of their victim story, getting a *no* regarding needing to know more information is Spirit's way of swaying them from mentally picking at any former wounds—which would only reactivate the energetic vibration. It allows for whatever was cleared and released to remain cleared and released—and this supports the transformational process.

Divining for More Information Protocol

- Ask: *Do I need to know more information about this (in the context of the statement you are focusing on) at this time?* Divine.

- If you receive a *no* response about needing to know additional information, proceed to the protocols for the clearing modality indicated.

- If you receive a *yes* response, ask something like:

  ○ *What information do I need to know at this time?*

  ○ Use your intuition to be open to information to appear to you in the form of signs, symbols, words, colors, sounds, the experience of emotions, and so on.

- Ask if the issue was inherited. If you get a *yes*:

  ○ Ask: *What additional information do I need to know at this time?* For example: maternal or paternal side? Male or female?

  ○ Use your intuition to be open to information to appear to you in the form of signs, symbols, words, colors, sounds, the experience of emotions, and so on.

  ○ Make a notation on the chart's *Challenged* box of an inherited energetic.

Chapter 22

Step 5: Eliminate Through
Energetic Clearing and Releasing

Learn to seek, trust, and follow your internal
God Guidance System (GGS)—also known as your intuition.
—Dr. Linda Humphreys

I believe that God / Spirit / Highest Power offers us an abundance of tools with which to liberate ourselves from our inner prison of negative subconscious (and sometimes conscious) thoughts, energy, and vibrations that can cause energetic blocks and imbalances in all areas of our lives. Set your intention to heal, use your divining skills, and allow the Divine to assist with your energetic clearings and releasings, God Mind consciousness expansion, and spiritual upliftment.

What's Next

Now that you have uncovered specific statements / thoughts / energy / vibrations that are in your subconscious—and, perhaps, your conscious—*and* your energy field, it is time for you to release these energetic blocks / imbalances / vibrations. This step addresses how to go about doing that.

I used specific modalities that I found extremely effective in releasing energetic blocks and imbalances with my own "GOD Project." Over the years I have studied numerous subconscious / unconscious, emotional and energetic clearing and releasing modalities. I have even become certified in several methods. Additionally, I have been inspired to create additional techniques and protocols.

I will share two modalities in this chapter. The first is what I call the ***Brow, Crown, and Down*** method; the second I call the

Acu-Points Rub / Tap method. Neither is superior to the other; they are just the two that have worked for me and were easy for my clients to learn. For your "GOD Project," you discern which clearing and releasing modality resonates with you.

NOTE: There may be some emotional energy releases (tears, crying, laughing) during the clearing and release process. If this should happen, it simply means that e-motion (energy in motion) is occurring.[8] During my own "GOD Project," sometimes I experienced dreamlike images and intuitive impressions, felt the energy of certain emotions, experienced sounds and colors, and received inner messages. Other times, I did not notice experiencing any of the above.

Divining Which Clearing Modality to Use
Protocol (detailed)

- Use divining to discern which clearing and releasing modality would be best for you to use at this time.
    - *Brow, Crown, and Down*? (Y / N?)
    - *Acu-Points Rub / Tap*? (Y / N?)
    - **NOTE**: If you test *no* (*weak*) for both, discern which other modality (for example, one you may be familiar with and have experience with) to use by using your intuition and divining.

- After receiving the indication of which modality to use at this time, ask:

    - *Is it safe and supportive for me to continue at this time?* Divine.

- If *yes*, continue. If you get a *no*—stop!

- Refer to *What to Do If You Get a No (Weak) to Proceed* on pages 139–140.

---

[8] If you do not experience a noticeable emotional release, it does not mean that a clearing and release did not occur. You can always verify a clearing through divining.

Brow, Crown, and Down

This is the modality to use if, via divining, you tested *yes* (*strong*) regarding the ***Brow, Crown, and Down*** clearing and releasing modality.

Tools

Both your fingertips and a magnet emit and carry electromagnetic energy, so your tools consist of:

- Your fingertips

- Optional: magnet (This can be a refrigerator magnet.)

Energy Clearing and Release Protocol for All Sessions

- Follow the ***Beginning Session Protocol for All Divining Sessions.***

- Follow ***Divining Statements Protocol.***

- Follow ***Divining for More Information Protocol.***

- Follow ***Divining Which Clearing Modality to Use Protocol***

- If the ***Brow, Crown, and Down Method*** is indicated, proceed.

Energetic Clearing and Release Procedures for a "Negative / Challenged Statement"[9]

This is the procedure to use if, when divining, you test *strong* (*yes*) regarding a "Negative / Challenged Statement." (This indicates there is resonance between you and the negative / challenged energetic.)

- Using your fingertip(s), begin by either lightly rubbing in a circle (for a few seconds—approximately five to six small circles) or tapping (approximately five to six times) on the third eye area (area between eyebrows and in the center of

---

[9]   If the statement energetic is inherited, refer to ***Clearing and Releasing Inherited Energy Protocol for All Statements (Brow, Crown, and Down)*** on pages 146-147.

the forehead). Proceed rubbing or tapping at various spots along the meridian line up to your crown (top of the head) and down (the back of your head to behind your neck). Rub or tap along the path described.

- Modifications:
  - Sweep your fingertips along the Brow, Crown, and Down meridian pathway instead of rubbing or tapping. Sweep several times. (I tend to sweep five or six times.)
  - Sweep the magnet instead of rubbing or tapping. Sweep several times.

- At the same time, state (verbally or silently) one or more of the following statements:
  - "Release. Release. Release."
  - "Be gone. Be gone. Be gone."
  - "I Am free! I Am free! I Am free!"
  - Or create something to that effect.

NOTE: For me, either lightly rubbing about three to six circles, tapping three to six times per point along the meridian path, or swiping the magnet or fingertips three to six times along the meridian path is sufficient most of the time; other times it takes more than six times. When uncertain, I divine to discern how many circular rubs / taps / swipes are best. It may vary from time to time. Follow your intuition.

Clearing and Releasing Inherited Energy Protocol for All Statements (Brow, Crown, and Down Method)

If there is an indication for you to divine for more information and there is an indication that the energy / vibration was inherited,

- Send a blessing to your ancestor while simultaneously doing more Brow, Crown, and Down rubs / taps / sweeps— more times than you usually would—and the amount you are intuitively guided to do and / or the amount you discern via divining.

- Additionally, rub or tap more acu-points along the meridian path.

  ○ Visualize a cord being untied, a chain broken, a lock opening between you and your ancestor as it relates to that specific statement—or whatever image comes forward for you.

  ○ You can also state things like:

    ■ "Release and go in peace,"
    ■ "I honor and bless you. Be at peace. Now release."
    ■ Or whatever you feel your intuition is guiding you to state.

Confirm the Energetic Clearing and Release

- Ask: *Has this been released?* Divine.

- If you get a *strong* (*yes*) response, confirm the release.

How to Confirm the Release of a "Negative / Challenged Statement" Energetic Protocol

- Say the statement (either verbally or silently) and then divine again.

  ○ You should test *weak* (*no*).

- If you test *weak* (*no*) to the "Negative / Challenged Statement,"

  ○ Ask: *Is it safe and supportive for me to continue at this time?* Divine.

  ○ If you get a *strong* (*yes*) response, continue.

NOTE: If you still get a *strong* (*yes*) response to the "Negative / Challenged Statement"—stop!

- Ask: *Is it safe and supportive for me to continue at this time?* Divine.
- If you get a *strong (yes)* response,
  - Restate your intention to release the "Negative / Challenged" energetic.
  - Rub, tap, or sweep more times.
    - › Remember: If this was an inherited energetic, the clearing and releasing will require more rubs / taps / swipes.
  - Say the statement (either verbally or silently) and then divine again.
    - › You should test *weak (no)*.

Another NOTE: If you still test *strong (yes)* for the "Negative / Challenged Statement" energetic or get a *weak (no)* response after asking if it is safe and supportive to continue at this time, follow the same protocols explained in *What to Do If You Get a No (Weak) to Proceed* on pages 139–140.)

Energetic Clearing and Release Procedures for a "Lack of Positive Statement"[10]

This is the procedure to use if, when divining, you test *weak (no)* regarding a "positive" ("Lack of Positive") statement using the *Brow, Crown, and Down* method. (This indicates there is dissonance / non-resonance between you and the positive energetic.)

- While rubbing or tapping on each meridian point, say (verbally or silently)—following your Intuition / Inner Guidance regarding which statement to say, when to say it, and so on—one or all of the following statements:
  - "It is safe for me to experience _____."
    Example: "It is safe for me to experience God's love of me."

---

[10] If the statement energetic is inherited, refer to *Clearing and Releasing Inherited Energy Protocol for All Statements (Brow, Crown, and Down)* on pages 146-147.

- ○ "I welcome the energy of _____ now."
  Example: I welcome the energy of God's love for me now.
- ○ "It is for my maximum benefit to accept and experience _____ now."
  Example: "It is for my maximum benefit to accept and experience God's love for me now."
- ○ And / or whatever else you feel, intuitively, to state.

- Also, you can specifically address the blocks and / or imbalances:

  - ○ "It is safe for me to remove all blocks and imbalances toward experiencing _____ now."
  - ○ And / or something similar. Follow your intuition.

Confirm the Clearing and Release

- Ask: *Has this been released?* Divine.

- If you get a *strong* (*yes*) response, confirm the release.

How to Confirm the Release of a "Lack of Positive Statement" Energetic Protocol

- Say the statement (either verbally or silently) and then divine again.

- You should test *strong* (*yes*) for the "positive" statement energetic.

- If you test *strong* (*yes*) to the statement,

  - ○ Ask: *Is it safe and supportive for me to continue at this time?* Divine.
  - ○ If you get a *strong* (*yes*) response, continue.

NOTE: If you still get a *weak* (*no*) response to the "positive" statement—stop!

  - ○ Ask: *Is it safe and supportive for me to continue at this time?* Divine.

- ○ If you get a *strong* (*yes*) response,
    - ▪ Restate your intention to release the "Lack of Positive" energetic.
        - ❯ Remember: If the statement's energetic / vibration is inherited, refer to ***Clearing and Releasing Inherited Energy Protocol for All Statements (Brow, Crown, and Down Method)***

- • Say the statement (either verbally or silently) and then divine again.
    - ○ You should get a *strong* (*yes*) response.

Another NOTE: If you still test *weak* (*no*) for the "positive" statement energetic or get a *weak* (*no*) response after asking if it is safe and supportive to continue at this time, refer to ***What to Do If You Get a No (Weak) to Proceed.*** (See pages 139–140.)

Always remember: Be gentle and patient with yourself. Drink lots of water. Try again another day.

Acu-Points Rub / Tap Method

Releasing energy via acu-points takes many different forms, and each form does things in slightly different ways. Some of the formal systems using tapping on acu-points are Thought Field Therapy (TFT), Tapas Acupressure Technique (TAT), and Emotional Freedom Technique (EFT).

Just as acupuncture and acupressure redirect energy via the meridian channels, so does lightly rubbing in a circular motion and / or tapping on various meridian channel points / acu-points. Though each tapping technique varies in the number of tapping points and the phrasing of release statements, all involve tapping specific points on the body.

For myself and with my clients, via divining I discern which statements need to be addressed. Next, if the ***Acu-Points Rub / Tap Method*** is indicated as the clearing and release modality best suited at the time of testing, these are the steps I follow:

Tools

- Fingertips
- Awareness of some meridian acu-points: (partial listing)
  - top of the head (crown)
  - "third eye" area (center forehead above eyebrows)
  - temple / next to the eye
  - under the eye
  - under the nose / above the lip
  - under the ear
  - middle of the chin
  - below the collarbone / below where the collarbone sticks out
  - front side of armpits
  - sides of rib cage
  - side of palm (below index finger)
  - web between index finger and thumb
  - wrist (hug with opposite hand)

NOTE: Not all of these acu-points need to be rubbed in a circular motion or tapped. Additionally, other points can be rubbed or tapped. First, practice doing all of them. Some systems use more, some use less. I tend to rub or tap the following: crown, brow area, side of the eye, under the eye, under the nose / above the lip, middle of chin, below the collarbone, side of palm, index / thumb web (sometimes), and hugging the wrist of one hand with the other hand. Sometimes I rub or tap additional areas; sometimes I rub or tap very few areas.

Simply stated, rubbing or tapping releases the energetic hold your subconscious / unconscious mind uses to keep the thought / vibration in place within your mind and energy field. I believe the rubbing or tapping is a type of energetic pattern disruption.

Energy Clearing and Release Protocol for All Sessions

- Follow *Beginning Session Protocol for All Divining Sessions.*

- Follow *Divining Statements Protocol.*

- Follow *Divining for More Information Protocol.*

- Follow *Divining Which Clearing Modality to Use Protocol.*

- If *Acu-Points Rub / Tap Method* is indicated, proceed.

Energetic Clearing and Release Procedures for a "Negative / Challenged Statement" [11]

This is the procedure to use if, when divining, you test *strong* (*yes*) regarding a "Negative / Challenged Statement" and are guided to use the *Acu-Points Rub / Tap Method*.

- Using your fingertips, begin lightly rubbing or tapping (five or six circular rubs or taps ... or as many times as you are intuitively directed to rub or tap, or however long it takes for you to complete one of the statements below) on the meridian points suggested or indicated.

- While rubbing or tapping on each point, say (verbally or silently)—following your Intuition / Inner Guidance regarding which statement to say, when to say it, and so on—one or all of the following statements:

  - "Release. Release. Release."
  - "I release this energy from me now."
  - "Time to let this go."
  - "It is safe for me to let this go now."
  - Or say whatever else you feel, intuitively, you want to state.

---

[11] If the statement energetic is inherited, refer to *Clearing and Releasing Inherited Energy Protocol for All Statements (Acu-Points Rub / Tap Method)* on page 153.

NOTE: For me, most of the time it would take about three to six circular rubs or taps per point; other times it would take more than six. When uncertain, I would divine to discern how many circular rubs or taps would be best. It may vary from time to time. Follow your intuition.

Clearing and Releasing Inherited Energy Protocol (Acu-Points Rub / Tap Method)

If there was an indication for you to divine for more information and there was an indication that the energy / vibration was inherited, do more acu-point rubs / taps—more times than you usually would—and the amount that you are guided to do. Additionally, it may be beneficial to rub or tap more acu-points.

- At the same time, send a blessing to your ancestor.

- Visualize a cord being untied, a chain broken, a lock opening between you and your ancestor as it relates to that specific statement, or whatever else comes forward for you.

- You can also state things like:
  - "Release and go in peace."
  - "I honor and bless you. Be at peace. Now release."
  - Or whatever you feel your intuition is guiding you to state.

Confirm the Clearing and Release

- Refer to *How to Confirm the Release of a "Negative / Challenged Statement" Energetic Protocol*. (See pages147–148.)

Energetic Clearing and Release Procedures for a "Lack of Positive Statement"[12]

This is the procedure to use if, when divining, you test *weak (no)* regarding a "positive" statement using the *Acu-Points Rub/Tap Method*.

- While rubbing or tapping on each point, say (verbally or silently)—following your Intuition/Inner Guidance regarding which statement to say, when to say it, and so on—one or all of the following statements:

    ○ "It safe for me to experience _____."
    Example: "It is safe for me to experience God's love."

    ○ "I welcome the energy of _____ now."
    Example: "I welcome the energy of God's love for me now."

    ○ "It is for my maximum benefit to accept and experience _____ now."
    Example: "It is for my maximum benefit to accept and experience God's love for me now."

    ○ And/or whatever else you feel, intuitively, to state.

- Also, you can specifically address the blocks and/or imbalances:

    ○ "It is safe for me to remove all blocks and imbalances toward experiencing _____ now."

    ○ And/or something similar. Follow your intuition.

Confirm the Clearing and Release

- Refer to *How to Confirm the Release of a "Lack of Positive Statement" Energetic Protocol.* (See pages 149–150.)

---

[12] If the statement energetic is inherited, refer to *Clearing and Releasing Inherited Energy Protocol for All Statements (Acu-Points Rub/Tap Method)* on page 153.

Other Energetic Clearing Modalities and Sources of Information

As mentioned earlier, you may be directed to use an additional or a different clearing and releasing modality or modalities. As always, use your Intuition / Inner Guidance and divine to discern which modality would be most beneficial at the time and each time you do this work. The modality you are directed to use may vary from session to session. It is important that you always check within.

Again, other sources of information include directly asking God / Spirit / Highest Power and by using your intuition. Affirm clarity. Always ask for guidance and support.

NOTE: When the time comes to do the clearing and release process, there may be times when you will be able to clear and release multiple statements; other times you'll only clear and release one or two. Be patient with yourself and with your process.

See *GETTING GOD*™ ~ *The Guidebook—Exploration & Conscious Connection Support for Your "GOD Project"* for specific examples and session suggestions.

Chapter 23

Step 6: Empower

Don't ask yourself what the world needs. Ask yourself what makes you come alive, and go do that, because what the world needs is people who have come alive.

—*Howard Thurman*

At this point in your "GOD Project," I want to offer suggestions to support you in positively reinforcing and shoring up any and all new and "positive" perspectives regarding God / Spirit / Highest Power and your perceived relationship with God. Below are all things I have used and have found to be successful for reinforcing lessons learned, insights gleaned, and relationship "improvements" (on my part).

Supportive "GOD Project" Relationship Practices

Maintaining a positive relationship—with anyone—requires time, energy, effort, positive focus, commitment, devotion, communication, and honesty, just to name a few key elements. The same is true as it relates to improving your perceived relationship with God.

Here are some ways I have incorporated these elements.

- Meditating—listening to God.
- Journaling—expressing my thoughts, feelings, and ideas.
- Writing positive affirmations.
- Setting my intentions, upon waking, regarding my perceived relationship with God.
- Upon waking, expressing gratitude.

- Prior to sleeping, expressing gratitude.

- Also prior to sleeping, setting my intention to enable my subconscious mind to relax during my sleep time and to enable blocks and / or imbalances to be cleared and released in an easy and gentle manner—and to wake refreshed and invigorated.

- Socializing with energetically and spiritually uplifting people.

- Getting additional support on all levels. Some examples:
  - Spiritual: seeking spiritual counseling, prayer support
  - Seeking additional energetic healing

Regardless of your religion or denomination, here are some things you can do to support yourself in connecting to God Within and God Throughout:

- Chant, recite mantras

- Sing or listen to spiritually uplifting songs

- Listen to spiritually based inspirational and uplifting recordings

- Attend spiritually based inspirational and uplifting workshops, seminars, and training programs

While more suggestions and support materials can be found in *GETTING GOD™ ~ The Guidebook—Exploration & Conscious Connection Support for Your "GOD Project,"* what is listed above will be supportive ... and a great start.

Real joy comes when we get the right desire met—the desire for God, for a life led by the Spirit, fulfilling not our material desires but our deepest need, which is to be in a close relationship with our Creator. That is the source of true blessing. The only source.

— *Michael W. Smith*

Afterword

Both during and after completing my "GOD Project," I observed a myriad of different experiences, emotions, and results. While experiences will vary for each and every person who utilizes this program, I hope this section will shed some light on potential things you may or may not experience—although there are no promises or guarantees.

Generally, if there was a "negative / challenged" vibration statement (as it related to God), I tested strong for it. While this is a huge exaggeration, I do believe I had many layers—and layers upon layers—to clear and release. It took me a while to complete this process.

There were times during the clearing and releasing process that I burst out in tears. It was, as I experienced it, simply a release of old and stuck energy. I felt lighter (not so burdened or stressed) after the release. Sometimes I felt tired and had to take a nap.

My "Big Kahuna" Session

One time, after having completed multiple sessions and having cleared and released the energetic vibration of multiple "Negative / Challenged Statements," one particular statement (and its subsequent clearing and release) was extremely impactful. During the clearing process, within my God Mind's "eye," I "saw," from a neutral perspective, something that some people would label as a past life experience. Actually, I clearly remember several very different "lifetime" scenarios passing through my awareness. The common thread I experienced while witnessing this was that I had died (multiple times) extremely angry—even enraged.

I was angry at God for not "saving" me, not "smiting mine enemies." (That archaic phrase is / was something I would never routinely nor consciously ever say, yet it came forward during the clearing and releasing session.) The lesson: I chose to die angry—at God.

Yet in watching all of this unfold and happen, I saw and experienced that *God was actually there the entire time—in and throughout all of it—and God was within everyone involved in those situations as well.*

The problem was *me!* *I* was the one who chose not to see God around and within me and within "mine enemy." God was there the entire time: around all, in all, and as all. *I* was the one who turned away from that Truth. *I* was the one who created the blocks and barriers of separation and of against-ness toward God.

I sobbed … deeply … for a very, very long time.

I felt as if, with every sob, I was releasing stagnant energy from a deep, deep, deep place within. It was so deep and profound that I was rendered practically speechless for three days. I was in surrender. I was in profound awe, humility … and gratitude.

While all of this was going on, I had a visceral experience of what I now know was (and have experienced since then as well) to be the True Nature of God: loving, adoring, patient, profoundly welcoming, compassionate, always present, deeply caring, comforting … just to name a few.

I also experienced a profound sense and understanding of "The Oneness": I could see God in each situation (as in: on the battle fields of wars) and in everyone—including "mine enemy." Again, God is around all, in all, and as all.

On a mental level, when I think back to what happened, I experienced a remarkable absence of any iota of judgment, punishment, anger, shame, separation, unworthiness, or a feeling of being less than—in a negative way—to name just a few.

Believing in Past Lives—*Not* Required

At this time, it is important that you know that "believing in past lives" is *not* a requirement, a prerequisite, nor requisite to doing this work and receiving value from doing your own "GOD Project." I am simply sharing with you what I experienced. I cannot give a logical explanation for my experience of seeing images that I did not experience in this lifetime. I am not going to defend whether or not this was a "true" past life experience or not. Any / all stories are not important.

What Really Matters

This is what matters: I experienced some negative / separation energy inside of me—between God and myself. I made a conscious and deliberate (intentional) decision to clear and release it via my "GOD Project." What *is* important is the direct, intimate, and profoundly loving experience of God and of God's True Nature.

The capital "T" Truth—as I experienced it:

- Negative energy was released.

- "Stories" are not important.

- This was not a mental "processing" experience.

- I do not need to mentally "figure this out."

- The clearing and releasing were real, visceral, and profound for me.

- I experienced clearing and releasing—on all levels.

I noticed positive shifts and a lightening / lifting of negative energy—especially compared to what I formerly experienced when I would think about my relationship with God. After about three weeks of doing daily clearing and releasing sessions, something profound happened. By clearing the energy associated with one particular "Negative / Challenged Statement" of a feeling / misperception I had about God, I felt a surge of energy come forward. It felt as if by clearing that one particular negative energy statement, a multitude of other "negative / challenged" energetic blocks and imbalances were simultaneously cleared and released. I had hit my inner "big kahuna"—the lynchpin that held a massive amount of separation energy within me toward God.

My mind wants to "reason" that multiple clearings and releasing happened at once because, perhaps, the vibrations were attached at the same time—or perhaps they might have carried similar vibrations. It actually does not matter. Again, this not a mental process. No "story" or "figuring it out" is necessary or required. Actually, the creation of further stories only befuddles things by keeping me in my thinking mind. Knowing that to be true for myself and what I tended to do, I decided to simply own and embrace the clearing and releasing with gratitude. I suggest you do the same.

I have been asked numerous times why I could not or did not just find that one statement to begin with. This is what I have discovered: Clearing and releasing is meant to be an easy and gentle process. By discerning (via asking within and divining) which energetic statement "needs" or "wants" to be cleared first, next, and so on, I believe it lays the groundwork for a more gentle, graceful, and grace-filled unfoldment and process.

Through doing this kind of work for a while, I also discovered that some energetic blocks and imbalances need to be cleared and released first and before all others—especially before the more deeply imbedded and entrenched blocks and imbalances can be cleared and released. I believe the initial clearings serve as "gatekeepers."

When the "gatekeepers" experience gentle clearing and releasing, it signals the psyche / ego that everything is fine—that it can relax a bit and it is "safe" to do this process. This then paves the way for other subconscious / unconscious "negative" energy blocks to ease up a bit, loosen their grip, and gently rise to the surface. It is almost as if each "gatekeeper" tests the waters—to see if it can trust the process. The experience of a gentle process eases the psyche / ego and it does not feel "threatened." It senses it will be not "destroyed" or "annihilated"; it will be "safe"; all is well—all will be well—and all can be even better.

All parts of this process have a purpose: the constant checking within by asking, via divining—"Is it safe and supportive to continue at this time?" … "Has this been released?"—and asking if more information is needed or wanted to be revealed; *plus* giving the hurt or wounded aspects inside respect, care, compassion, attention, and loving. This is the means—the process—which assists in allowing the "gatekeepers" to relax—allowing the gates (which are keeping the "negative" / "lack of positive" energetics in place within) to open for clearing and releasing. I would even venture to say that a lack of the above (compassion, loving, respect, and so on) were most likely the reasons the energy became stuck in the first place. By embracing loving compassion and not making the energetic block and / or imbalance *wrong* or *bad*, it allowed the miracle I experienced to happen.

One surprising discovery came as a result of doing my "GOD Project." Prior to the commencement of my "Project," I tested myself, using the same method that Dr. David R. Hawkins used, to discern what level of consciousness I started with (according to the "Map of Consciousness" from his book *Power vs. Force*). I also tested myself after the completion of the major portion of my "GOD Project." The before-and-after results were astounding. Not only did my score increase but it catapulted in a dramatic and astonishing way.

On some level, I hesitated sharing this because I do not want what I shared to be misconstrued or misused. I have found that in some religious and metaphysical circles, some people emit an air of what I call "spiritual superiority." It is akin to a "holier than thou" attitude. I do not want to inadvertently instigate a "What's *your* score?" mental and ego comparison, which could, in turn, become a system in which people establish and assert a hierarchy (in which they are superior in their mental / ego-minds). I do not want someone's score to be used as a weapon between and among themselves and others. Additionally, I do not want someone's score—or more specifically—someone's potentially negative view of their own score—to be turned within and used as a spiritual, mental, emotional, and psychological weapon against themselves. This will only add fuel to their mental / ego-minds and will reinforce thoughts, feelings, and misperceptions of inferiority. I do, however, believe that the benefits of increasing one's consciousness level (experience of greater inner peace, harmony, The Oneness, and so on)—and not the actual score itself, is what is significant and important to share.

My "GOD Project" will never end. As time passes, I still find some feelings and thoughts to clear and release, which I do on a regular basis. I release when they appear. Hopefully, you will do the same.

Another important aspect of my experience: Regardless of what I am emotionally experiencing and physically feeling on any given day, I now know that God's love is real, ever-present, and powerful. I truly experienced my mantra:

"I know that I know that I know—
I *Am* a beloved daughter of God, in whom God is well pleased."

I know this is True for myself.
I know this is True for you.
I Am Grateful! I Am Grateful! I Am Grateful!
And so it is …
Namaste.

Summary:
Divining Steps
and
Energy Clearing and Releasing Protocols

Below you will find a list of steps and protocols that can assist you with the divining process and with the energetic clearing and releasing during your "GOD Project." (See pages 137-155 for detailed information.)

- *Beginning Session Protocol for All Divining Sessions* (pp. 137-138)

- *Establish Your Baselines* (p. 138)

- *Divining Statements Protocol* (pp. 140-141)

- *Divining for More Information Protocol* (p. 142)

- *Divining Which Clearing Modality to Use* (p. 144)

- *Energy Clearing and Release Protocol for All Sessions* (p. 145)

  - *Energetic Clearing and Release Procedures for "Negative / Challenged Statements"[13]* (pp. 145-146)

  - *Energetic Clearing and Release Procedures for "Lack of Positive Statements"[14]* (pp. 148-149)

- *Confirm the Energetic Clearing and Release* (p. 147)

  - *How to Confirm the Release of a "Negative / Challenged Statement"* (pp. 147-148)

  - *How to Confirm the Release of a "Lack of Positive Statement"* (pp. 148-149)

---

[13] If necessary, refer to the *Clearing and Releasing Inherited Energy Protocol for All Statements* on pages 146-147.

[14] If necessary, refer to the *Clearing and Releasing Inherited Energy Protocol for All Statements* on pages 146-147.

Bibliography

Airodyssey.net. "Inflight Passenger Instructions."
    Accessed March 7, 2017.
    https://airodyssey.net/reference/inflight.

Bibleinfo.com. "What Are the Seven Deadly Sins?" Bible Questions.
    Accessed March 2, 2017.
    www.bibleinfo.com.

Brennan, Barbara Ann. *Hands of Light: A Guide to Healing through the Human Energy Field.* New York: Bantam Books, 1988.

Chakras.info. "The 7 Chakras." Accessed February 7, 2017.
    www.chakras.info.

DeMille, Cecil, dir. *The Ten Commandments.* 1956. Hollywood: Paramount, 1999. DVD.

Dispenza, Joe. *Breaking the Habit of Being Yourself: How to Lose Your Mind and Create a New One.* San Diego: Hay House, 2012. Kindle edition.

Edwards, Jonathan, and Smolinski, Reiner, ed. "Sinners in the Hands of an Angry God. A Sermon Preached at Enfield, July 8th, 1741." Sermon, Enfield, 1741. Electronic Texts in American Studies, 54.
    http://digitalcommons.unl.etas/54.

Erickson, Alexa. "20 Quotes by Rumi that Will Make You Feel the Love." *Collective Evolution.* Last modified October 29, 2013.
    www.collective-evolution.com.

Goodreads.com. "Quotes." Accessed November 14, 2016.
    www.goodreads.com.

Hawkins, David R. *Power vs. Force: The Hidden Determinants of Human Behavior, Author's Official Revised Edition.* San Diego: Hay House, 2012. Kindle edition.

Heriot, Drew, dir. *The Secret.* 2006. Australia, Primetime Productions, 2006. DVD.

The Holy Bible: King James Version. Last accessed Nov 14, 2016. http://biblehub.com.

Horan, Ellamay, and Newton, Wm. L. *The Illustrated Revised Edition of Baltimore Catechism No. 1.* New York: W.H. Sadler, Inc., 1944.

Jung, C. G. *Dreams.* Translated by R.F.C. Hull. Princeton: Princeton University Press, 1974.

Kelley, Bennet. *Saint Joseph First Communion Catechism.* New York: Catholic Book Publishing Co., 1963.

King James Bible with VerseSearch: Red Letter Edition (Kindle Locations 39277-39280). Seattle: Amazon Digital Services LLC: 2013. Kindle edition.

Lamsa, George M. *Holy Bible: From the Ancient Eastern Text.* New York: HarperCollins, 1933. Kindle edition.

Luton, Frith. "Carl Jung Projections." Frithluton.com. Accessed March 2, 2017.
http://frithluton.com.

Martino, Joe. "20 Profound Quotes by Carl Jung that Will Help You to Better Understand Yourself." *Collective Evolution.* Last modified January 25, 2016.
www.collective-evolution.com.

Mollon, Phil. "Thought Field Therapy and Its Derivatives: Rapid Relief of Mental Health Problems Through Tapping on the Body." *Primary Care and Community Psychiatry* 12, no. 3–4 (December 2007): 2–6. doi: 10.1080/17468840701750836.

Newton, John. *Amazing Grace*. Timeless Truths Free Online Library. Accessed March 3, 2017. http://library.timelesstruths.org.

"Quotes of Michelangelo." Michelangelo Paintings, Sculptures, Biography. Accessed March 3, 2017. www.michelangelo.org.

Shen-Nong Limited. "Meridians." Shen-Nong.com. Accessed February 27, 2017. www.shen-nong.com.

Sister Annunziata. *Sister Annunziata's First Communion Catechism*. New York: Benziger Brothers, Inc., 1946.

"Sin." Wikipedia. Accessed July 31, 2018. https://en.wikipedia.org/wiki/Sin.

"The Structure and Function of a Healthy Spine: Cleveland Clinic." Accessed March February 27, 2017. https://my.clevelandclinic.org.

Tompkins, Peter, and Bird, Christopher. *The Secret Life of Plants*. New York: Harper & Row Publishers, Inc., 1973.

Walsch, Neal Donald. *Conversations with God: Book I.* Charlottesville, Virginia: Hampton Roads Publishing Company, Inc., 2012.

Williamson, Marianne. *A Return to Love: Reflections on the Principles of A Course in Miracles*. New York: Harper Collins, 1992.

Acknowledgments

Thank you
God / Spirit / My Higher Power—without whom I could not do
anything.
I am in awe, deeply humbled and grateful for
the miraculous positive transformations in my life.

To my teachers and "way-show-ers":
Dr. Seuss (aka: Theodor Seuss Geisel)
Abraham Lincoln
The Pathwork
Dr. Carl Rogers
Dr. Carl Jung
Marianne Williamson
A Course in Miracles
Rev. Dr. Martin Luther King, Jr.
Rev. Dr. Michael Beckwith
Dr. Paul Barrett
Conversations with God
Drs. Ron and Mary Hulnick
Dr. Caroline Myss
Dr. Joe Dispenza
Dr. Robert Holden

To my dear friends, who made me laugh—especially at myself.

To my "spiritual friends"—
my "nudge-rs" / "prodders" / "stackers" / "thorns in my side"
through whom I have learned some of my greatest spiritual lessons
along the way.
Y'all know who you are. ☺

To Jeff—
a source of an abundance of great love,
joy, fun, adventure, laughter, and support.

And, as always …
Thank you, BABY JESUS!!!

Amen.

About the Author

I am a seeker.

I am a perpetual student.

I make mistakes.

As a seeker and student, I have learned from my mistakes and am now making conscious strides to "choose again," as *A Course in Miracles* suggests.

I believe in releasing any / all perceived internal confines (judgments, misperceptions)—especially related to the past.

I believe in all forms of forgiveness—including self-forgiveness.

I believe in learning lessons, releasing the past—and moving on.

I believe in being grounded in the present moment because this is where the magic happens. I strive to be present—to fully show up and be "all in"—in all I do.

I believe in being more loving and compassionate toward myself and others in the present—which sets the tone for a more love-filled present—and paves the way for a more love-filled future.

I made a commitment to transform—on all levels.

I strive for personal excellence.

I believe in change, transformation, miracles, and the power of Love.

I view my transformed life as a miracle.

I made a commitment to support others in their transformation and support them in experiencing their own miracles.

My zodiac sign is Gemini.

My "birth card" is Ace of Clubs.

My Enneagram test revealed that I have many personality tendencies (with "tied" scores in both my number one and two positions)—with lots of "wings" to support me.

I don't expect other people to "figure me out" because I can't "figure" myself out.

I tell those I love to "strap on your seat belt" and enjoy the ride when they are with me.

I love flowers.
Tulips make me smile.
I love the scent of carnations.
Laughter makes me laugh.
I love to laugh.
I love spending time with friends.
I believe in "retail therapy."
I love new adventures.
I love delightful surprises.
I love traveling and meeting new people.
I love 70 percent dark chocolate, Utz Potato Chips, and eating
Maryland crab … anything.
I love to eat.

I love my various families, tribes, and peeps.
I love my husband.
I love America.
I love the entire universe.
I love children.
I love God.
I love "Baby Jesus."
I love you.

Linda Humphreys, PhD
www.DrLindaHumphreys.com

Index

marked, 88, 90
mild resistance,
133–36
maintaining,
133–34, 136
mind, x, 17, 23, 25,
27–29, 34–37, 42,
44, 48, 58, 64–65,
77–80, 101–2,
164–66, 168
busy, 79
chattering, 101
conscious, 43,
77–78
ego's, 79
monkey, 48, 55,
79, 101
munching, 79,
101, 141
unconscious, 78,
79, 151
mindset, xi, 114
following suc-
cess, 98, 114
miracles, 47, 49, 51,
54–55, 57, 97–98,
165, 170–72
miracles states, 54
misconceptions, xv
misinterpretation,
41
misperceiving, 78
misperceptions,
xiv–xvi, 13, 37,
39, 57, 68, 71–73,
101, 103, 119,
121–22, 163, 166,
172
modalities, 88–89,

143–45, 155
Modifications, 146
Most High, 58–59
mother, xii–xiii,
xvi, 17–18, 23–24,
117–18
earthly, 24
heavenly, 24, 42
spiritual, 54
Mother Mary, 24
motion, circular,
150–51
motivations, con-
scious, 3
movements,
marked, 88, 90
movies, 3, 17, 20,
94, 117
inspired, 34
Moving Forward,
102, 104
multiple clearings,
164
Multiple Minds,
77, 79
multi-sensory
stimulation, 4
muscles, 89–91, 138
micro, 88, 90
skeletal, 87, 89
muscle strain,
133–36
my will be done, 43

N

name, 4–5, 8, 15,
20, 53, 55, 65,
133–36, 157, 162
correct, 139

false, 134, 136
nature abhors a
vacuum, 37
negative associa-
tions, 78
Negative/
Challenged, 147
Negative/
Challenged
Statements,
126–27, 129, 145,
152
negative conse-
quences, 27
negative emotions,
27, 29, 36
negative energetic
block, 127
negative energy,
123, 163
clear, 122
negative energy
blocks, 164
negative energy
statement, 163
negative feelings,
39
negative patterns,
29
negative percep-
tions, 103, 119
negative persevera-
tions, 142
negative program-
ming, 37
negative reactions,
41, 104–5
negative responses,
104

www.ingramcontent.com/pod-product-compliance
Lightning Source LLC
Chambersburg PA
CBHW071945090426
42740CB00011B/1833